"My experience in the past 30 years in the fields of healthcare practitioner and investments is critically ever-changing and unpredictable. Making strategic choices became a swirling vortex until my introduction to Deborah's work, which rendered a stress-reducing, cognitive approach to making choices. More importantly, my emotional/mental and physical health improved in relationship to my newly acquired relationship to my internal dialog and attitudes, which became a friendly asset rather than foe. As my creative process has also woken up, I find my old structures of thinking and feeling have been replaced with positive motivation, intuition, and a new-found interest. Thank you, Deborah, for your cutting-edge brilliance."

—Kathleen Kennedy, Nicasio, CA

"Deborah has been a beacon of rare light in my transformation from fearful to fearless, since she began coaching me in 2002. I am an entertainment professional in film production, divorced, a single parent who has experienced depression and loss. Deborah has guided me through tough times with all these life issues and transitions, and coached me to see challenges as opportunities for growth. I have experienced hope, change, and joy by working with her. I recommend her to anyone who hopes to gain insight into themselves, improve relationships, and wants to think outside their comfort box and make wise career advancements."

—Paige Thomas, Albuquerque, NM

"Working with Deborah has taught me to live my life in a new way that is built on a foundation of acceptance and forgiveness. As a result of our work together, I am living my life from a place of much greater honesty, awareness, and accountability, and I feel empowered to use new tools that help me respond to life in a way that brings me better results in my personal and professional relationships. I have a new sense of freedom from patterns in my behavior that were not serving me, and I feel capable of creating my own happiness through the choices I make. I am truly grateful for Deborah's support and guidance. Working with Deborah has been a blessing to my growth."

—Teri Kelly, Novato, CA

"Working with Deborah Downey the last five years has totally changed my life! She motivates me with thoughtful questions asked with love and humor! Just knowing I am truly heard and have a true advocate in my corner is 'so empowering.' I always feel better after coaching with Deborah. Her coaching has validated and ignited me to take effective action and to make lasting changes in my life, professionally and personally. Deborah is an inspiration, an absolute blessing, and a true light on my path!"

—Alicia St. John, San Anselmo, CA

"Coach Deborah is a wonderful coach and mentor. She is patient, supportive, and kind. She knows how to inspire you to reach your goals, while making you laugh and have fun at the same time! I highly recommend Deborah to anyone who is looking to build their confidence and make a successful life for themselves. Coach Deborah has been an inspiration and a blessing in my life. Talking to her, I feel supported and understood. I am a sensitive person, and need someone who is gentle and kind, not harsh and abrupt. Whether you are stuck in your personal or professional life, or just need a very positive, wise, and unbiased person in your corner, I would encourage you to call Deborah and see for yourself how she can support and help you fulfill your dreams. What are you waiting for? With gratitude."

—Kirstin Ross, Los Angeles, CA

"Deborah Downey is a fantastic coach. She has literally saved my sanity by coaching me with ways to stay in the now through some pretty catastrophic life happenings. Without her, I'd be divorced, estranged from my troubled adult children, and crazy, I know it. To me, she has more to offer than Eckhart Tolle and Deepak Chopra combined. Maybe that's because she's all about utter and complete love, and she listens deeply to what is really going on with me. Together, she has helped me value and take care of myself and improved the quality of my life."

—Dee Harrington, Emeryville, CA

"Thanks to Deborah, I experienced tremendous personal growth. I started off with such a small agenda, not realizing what potential Deborah and I would have together. I wanted to get back my motivation for my lifetime projects. These were the books I had already written and was dragging my feet to successfully market. I knew I was blocked in some way. I started to realize how I was using my six-year cancer battle to block me from trying to reach my dreams. As the weeks passed, other things seemed so much bigger. Some of these other things were the wonderful people around me, and how maybe I wasn't truly showing how grateful I was for them. Gratitude. I needed a big dose of gratitude.

Then midway through our time-scheduled phone meetings, I was introduced to the concept of a higher power within me. I can't recall ever feeling as connected and strengthened. I never realized this higher power could help and comfort me. All I had to do was acknowledge this presence and ask for help now and then. My life is more on track now. I do the best I can do. When I can't do something alone, I ask for help. I have gratitude for the people around me and new found-strength, knowing I have connected the dots and found this higher power.

I don't need to find God in a church or a hymn or a prayer. I write my own prayers every day. I ask for help to be motivated and to learn and grow every day. My music is more inspired, as I play and teach piano and harp, and it has come time for me to begin giving back. Giving back has made me feel well again and given me boundless energy. I am hoping that the people who need to find me, will. I know I can help young piano and harp teachers with my books and teaching manuals (TeachingPianoMadeSimple.com). I practice gratitude daily and infuse all my activities with energy and enthusiasm. My higher power is helping me and I'm ready to give back. Thanks, Deborah, for these wonderful insights and for encouraging me to achieve all my potential. I'm lucky to know you—you are a very effective personal coach. This is a perfect calling for you. You are truly inspiring."

—Diane Phillips, Oak Park, CA

ABOUT THIS BOOK

Deborah Downey is a Certified Professional Life Coach and Dynamic Motivational Speaker and Author. She has 22 years experience coaching men and women of all ages, and shares her professional as well as personal insights in an easy-to-follow guide for readers seeking permanent lifetime healing. "25 Ideas That Will Forever Change Your Life" and "Life How-Tos" that focus on self-improvement by discussing self-care, confidence, learning how to connect and trust in your own highest power, letting go of shame and resentments, and becoming open and available to life. She guides you through "My Seven-Step System: How to Finally Find the Love of Your Life," based on her years of relationship coaching with men and women. Each step builds upon the last, and is designed to guide you to turn your dreams of partnership into reality.

This book offers techniques to transform daily worry and negativity into productive thinking. It gives you the tools you need to:

- improve relationships with your friends, family, and business associates

- become your own best ally

- actualize your dreams into reality

What Are You Worried About!

Peace of Mind
for Sensitive People
Living in an
Abrasive World

DEBORAH DOWNEY

Paperback ISBN: 978-1-939758-77-4
eBook ISBN: 978-1-939758-78-1

Library of Congress Control Number: 2014905571

For information contact:
Deborah Downey
(530) 902-7663
info@coachdeborahdowney.com

CONTENTS

PREFACE

IN THE SUMMER of 2002, while standing on the main floor of my split-level home in Southern California, I had just come up from the floor below where my mother was living, and stopped. I noticed while pausing there, I was right behind a supporting post that ran floor-to-ceiling and was about 8 to 10 inches wide. This post blocked my amazing, unobstructed view of the Pacific Ocean. I saw that if I stood a few inches to the right or the left of this post that the horizon revealed a speedboat coming from the left crossing through the waves to the right in front of me. None of this was apparent from behind the post. Considering this, I swayed and leaned from side to side a few more times. It occurred to me that I often live my life in the same manner from... behind a post. My post could be my own self-constructed emotional rut, or it could have been trained in me growing up to interpret the seemingly bad things that occur in life as problems when they really weren't. My conditioning and my positioning in life is a big part of how I experience my life. This experience became an exceptional moment in my life because I felt the presence of God. I realized that my Higher Power is always trying to show me more of my personal potential and more of my life's mission.

I understood right then that it's my limited experience and my arrogance that keeps me behind the post. This was the beginning of my awareness that I have options in life. I felt that I not only need to be willing to step right or left from where I cannot see, but I must also move constantly. I must continue to take action because my Higher Power won't force me to change or develop. It is my choice to grow spiritually.

Sometimes the posts fall down on their own or they burn down or they get knocked over by people or they even get ripped out by life itself. My point is... we don't have to wait: we can start today and decide to grow and cultivate our minds and enhance our life's potential. This option is what I call living by design instead of default. I invite you to take my hand and step away from your post.

My wish is to present several ideas in this book that can be used by you, my reader, to reclaim your thinking, and offer you new ideas and practices that can be put to use every day. I've noticed, however, that nothing changes just by reading a book. These simple ideas, if assimilated and consistently thought of, will bring you peace of mind, no matter what events happen in your life. My hope is that you will write each of the following ideas on squibs of paper, Post-its, or write them on your computer, and carry them around until you've integrated—internalized—them. These sometimes revolutionary ideas need to become second nature to you and counter any unsupportive ideas if they pop into your thinking. Please allow these new concepts to move from your head to your heart, no matter how long it takes.

I put them on a mirror in my car, in my checkbook, and in my wallet. I encourage you to discover your own positive and motivating ideas, too, and to write them down. I suggest taking one, two, or three of these ideas and focusing on them for a week or two apiece. Sharing them with others also helps. When others speak negative or unkind things, or feel the need to spread their doom and gloom perspective, listen patiently and leave when it feels right. Erase their drama from your thoughts. I tell myself, literally, "Erase, erase." I breathe in love and breathe out doubt and fear.

This book is about taking ownership of your own mind and getting it to support your highest self. It is not your business to teach or preach these beliefs to others.

As I always say, "Take what you like and leave the rest."

SECTION 1

About Me

Deborah and her husband, Ray, on the deck of their house, enjoying summertime

Deborah's house in the middle of winter, covered in snow

I WAS BORN on the East Coast in White Plains, New York. Today, I am a Certified Professional Life Coach/Dynamic Motivational Speaker and Author. I have twenty-two years' experience coaching men and women of all ages. What makes me special is the amount of personal growth I've achieved through the years of training, coaching, and mentoring I have been privileged to acquire.

I'm a fairly recent widow, and I've found love again three years after his transition. I am currently a newlywed. Just celebrated two years, and I'm more happy with my darling hubby, Ray, than I have been with any partner in my whole life.

Some of the things that you can expect to learn or benefit from would be that I would help you design your actions and your attitudes, instead of being at the mercy of other people's life formula or your own past history or your family's dysfunctional history. My work is deep work, and it has true, permanent healing for your lifetime.

With my coaching, you will learn how to take care of yourself, be comfortable and confident, learn how to connect and trust in your own Highest Power, let go of shame and resentments, be open and available to life, be creative as you've never been before, be intuitive, be your best self ever, be your own best ally, and know how to say no. You will feel confident about your choices. You will learn to be yourself and to bring joy to yourself, to your family, and your business associates. I will give you and share with you several techniques to keep fear and worry at bay every day.

Our egos and minds can be so hard on us. They can even be dangerous to go into alone. One of my clients said having me as her coach was like having a friendly, thinking mind to be her champion. Learning to turn down the chaos and find a clear channel is possible, and I will cheer you on. We all do so much better when we get positive affirmations and a friendly nonjudgmental ear to listen to us.

Your life is a precious gift and deserves to be supported, inspired, and positively challenged to keep growing.

I will guide you through my Seven-Step System designed to find love, as well as to share the ideas that will change your life. We will go deep, and discover your strengths and build on those, all those assets you already possess. The tools I share will be life-changing and provide a lifetime benefit. Your self-esteem and your ability to see life in a positive way, see your future in abundance and filled with opportunities, will become an organic process for you. You will wear life and joy like a loose garment. Please check out my website, **CoachDeborahDowney.com,** and join me on this journey to happiness.

How I Work With Clients and Whom I Love to Help

My first passion is to help singles find true love. I have my signature Seven-Step System designed to help them Finally Find the Love of Their Life! I found my true love and want to help others of all ages and genders find their special One. My programs and one-on-one coaching make their dating campaign fun and best of all successful!

Once the relationship is forged and the day-to-day stresses wear on a couple's nerves, I have more coaching practices to keep the fire and fun in your connection going indefinitely. I teach secrets of lovemaking and healthy techniques for communication and tools for handling conflict. If you really want to enjoy your life and live without regrets and resentments, I can teach you how to embrace each day with your partner drama free for the rest of your life!

I work with people who are tired of sabotaging themselves and who want to live without worry in their lives. I am passionate about helping people who want to be free of unhealthy habits and worn–out, useless thinking or people who want to feel like a success in all areas of their lives again.

Over the past twenty-five years, I have developed several concepts and techniques to help myself and those I've coached to have enjoyable, amazing, prosperous lives full of passion. I have worked with people of all walks of life and a variety of ages and genders to find their gifts and achieve their dreams. I am often praised as "very patient and intuitive." People say I have much kindness and wisdom to share, plus a lively sense of humor. I am most noted for my uncanny way of helping clients give up all forms of worry.

If you choose to coach with me, your life will change for the better in a very short time. What you take away from our sessions will bring you self-mastery and complement your unique brand of personal power, and all the ensuing acquired results will be long-lasting. I have many practical ideas, tools, and techniques you can use to enjoy and achieve your plans for the rest of your life.

I will help you discover your true worth and expect the best and get it. I predict with confidence you will be a joy to yourself and everyone you meet if you incorporate my ideas into your daily regimen. Life without fear and worry is a strong magnet that will pull whatever you desire your way. We will then explore all the methods you'll need to continue bringing you the results you desire.

Overcoming your obstacles, real or imagined, internal or external, and navigating these challenges that you will surely face can be much less stressful with my assistance and knowledge. I love helping people reach true brilliance as we work towards their goals and meet them!

Why Have a Higher Power

I WAS DIAGNOSED with multiple sclerosis in 1989 at the age of thirty-two. Even though it didn't stop me from becoming a cabaret star at my former 99-seat theatre in North Hollywood, every step I've taken over the last twenty-five years has been conscious. I cannot rush about or jump up and dash off. My only choice is to be in my body and plan my very next move. Do I envy people who can run and dance and climb mountains and wear high heels? You bet I do. And then I stop, and I lift my heart and my eyes in gratitude for all the rich insights and glorious attributes and blessings and the personal spiritual growth I have obtained because of living with MS. I do not believe Spirit gave me MS, but I feel My Divine Creator may have helped me by using my diagnosis to humble me. I am hopeful for the complete cure to be available in the next few years.

Why do I believe we could all live better with a Higher Power of our very own conception? I rely on God, a power greater than myself, for everything. I know this may mean nothing to some of you. That is your prerogative, of course, but relying solely on my own wits is a limited experience, whereas when I choose to use God as my employer, partner, mentor, teacher, nurturer, and inspiration, my life feels better.

So why have a power greater than yourself or use anything other than yourself to guide your decisions? Well, the main reason I call on God is that I don't trust my limited perspective. My thinking is generally self-seeking, self-serving, to be sure, and has been conditioned by society and history and many generations of fear and greed and the need to control to continue with that pattern. Today, I give myself permission to question my thoughts and actions, and ask where they came from and where they're leading me. I choose to use a loving Source that I understand as a complex set of values that leads to simply love and the love of life.

I feel for us all. Life today is moving so quickly, and there are endless opportunities to achieve massive amounts of income and personal growth, and yet difficult and painful awarenesses are shoved in our face about how our peoples of this earth suffer. It is largely due to all the remarkable technology that we are exposed to this information and must face reality on a daily basis, whether we choose to or not. Our economies, the need for control and power on a personal basis, and various governments around the globe, too, can all change rapidly day by day. Everything concerning our planet's survival and us and our families… all move at extreme speeds, all seemingly at the touch of a fingertip. People have grotesque amounts of income and assets, while other people die from starvation and lack of pure water. The disparity is staggering between the haves and the have-nots. This alone causes a tremendous chasm among peoples and fosters fear of not getting enough.

However, when it comes to peace of mind, it really does not matter where you are in the food chain or what possessions or position and status you have in life. It all seems to come down to our feelings and thoughts; they are what define our experience of what we can call our existence. We can be ignorant and unconscious and give our minds and emotions over to our governments, our parents, our spouses, our lovers, our children, our teachers, our employers, our prejudices and fears, our greed and our need to control others, and simply cross our fingers and shut our eyes and ears and just hope for the best. Throw caution to the wind as we sit in front of our new, giant-screen TV or play in bingo tournaments on our tablets and succumb to our cozy, slothful ways. Unless... you want to claim your glorious birthright and learn new ways of thinking and create a new life program with your Ultimate Partner, whom I choose to call God! You bet... it is all up to each of us to co-create with some help from Divine Love the life we were born to have. We have free will, and we may use it or we may cross our arms and sit back and let fate have her way with us. Or not. It's up to you! Your happiness, success, and failures are all on you. You have the gift of choice. You can manifest your heart's desires and live in Heaven while here on Earth. The blame game is over. Lay down your shame guns.

I assure you that my life experiences and my daily outlook have been far more glorious and rewarding since I became aware that I could improve my attitude and make solid, informed, and healthy actions in all areas of my life. My spirituality, personal finances, love relationships, creative endeavors, and my health—mind, body, and soul—have improved immeasurably since I declared my responsibility for how my life works. I decided to make my personal development my priority, and I've found this inward journey to be fascinating and truly rewarding despite setbacks and disasters—personal and global. I believe that through slow and consistent actions and humility, anyone can be wildly happy and successful by their own definition of what that is for them. I know lots of you have tried all sorts of teachers and mentors and even different faiths, and found yourselves more confused and feeling worse than when you lived in oblivion and hid out in a small, safe, yet boring, life. I will help you find your solutions that are crafted specifically for you and by you and The Master Diamond Cutter of us all.

SECTION 2

25 Ideas That Will Forever Change Your Life

1. *I Strive for Imperfection and I'm Always a Winner*

MOST PEOPLE LAUGH when I use this phrase—"I strive for imperfection, and I'm always a winner"—in a talk I give or when I coach them. Most likely because our society is forever challenging us to compete and compare with each other so we are constantly assessing how we're doing. This silly idea that I have to strive for imperfection is a reminder to me that I don't have to drive myself crazy with unattainable goals.

I notice that most of us do have hidden rules we carry from childhood that truly don't support us as adults. I find when I work with people, that with very little effort at all, we can take each rule and evaluate its validity and either release it or start living up to it.

When I first began understanding this phrase, I saw how there really isn't any way to be perfect for myself or for any other person who has ever lived. Therefore, to strive for something unattainable would be seeking failure, shame, and ultimately self-hatred. Juxtapose that outcome with being a winner and gaining freedom to be human and allowing for my messing up once in a while as a part of the process of living. I got it. My life will be less painful, shaming, and unproductive once I stop trying to be perfect. Only God is perfect in all ways.

No matter how well I do or how much I accomplish, I'll never be more than human. Finally, understanding the need for my own sense of perfection made me demand the same effort and standards of thought and action from everyone around me. Through self-examination, I began seeing myself as a witness of myself. It gave me that detachment to stand back and see myself. Discovering how to detach from previous events, and by simply looking at my patterns helped me observe periods of my life as if I were watching a movie with compassion and courage, instead of the uninformed, unforgiving critic I had whipped myself into believing that I should be. I knew from my work with many, many others that I am not unique, and that many people suffer from the unrealistic standard of perfection.

Once I accepted my innate imperfection, I was less inclined to beat myself up for my failings. A dear little Irishman named Tommy O'Meara would say, "If you make a mistake, forgive yourself. If you don't, you've made two." I don't need to beat myself up for being human.

My happiness is no longer tied to performance and accomplishment or outside circumstances. I do what I do because I love doing it. My happiness is an inside job. I know that no one can do a better me than me.

2. *My Opinion Isn't Always Required*

MY FRIEND, GINNY, a psychologist, said that to me, and it felt like an insult, and it stung a bit at the time. Then she explained what she meant. So now when some situation is potentially combative, or if I'm asked to comment on something that I feel is not really my business, or my problem, I usually find it is better for me not to say anything.

One of my clients, Betty, a lady in her late forties, was coaching with me to become more comfortable within herself, and also to learn how to be more effective in taking care of herself. Betty had a hard time learning how to take care of herself and asking for what she needed. One day, she came in and said that she'd said yes to hosting an engagement party for her best friend, and we discussed what she would say when her friend asked her for her blessing. Betty was really panicked about what she was going to say because, she confessed, she didn't like the fellow her buddy had picked to marry.

I told her, "Your opinion is not required," and her initial reaction was shock. And then she was relieved. Betty had thought that she had to have a position or a point of view for just about everything to appear intelligent and involved in life. Believing that her opinion was required was partly her ego, and its need for validation, and also partly for her fear of what others would think about her. Once I explained that it is perfectly okay to keep things to yourself, she was amazed and started laughing about how she wished she'd known that before dating her last boyfriend.

Betty hosted the party and changed the subject when her friend asked for her opinion. She told me it felt good to withhold her opinion, since she knew it would have little or no effect on her friend's actions or decisions. She liked the idea that she could have her private thoughts and not have to feel guilty if she didn't feel like sharing them. This one idea really empowered her, and her coaching took off. Her progress really took a giant step forward.

Many people feel obliged and suffocated by a need to justify who they are and what they stand for. Helping people take back their power is one of my favorite parts of coaching. Knowing our thoughts and actions do not require permission by others, and that by exercising our right to speak, or to decide not to comment, lets us decide what's best for us. Learning to keep my opinion to myself really helped me with my three grown children; everything from their choice of hairstyle and clothing, to the most critical choices in their partners has been off-limits for my comment or preference. It is simply none of my business. I let them know I want only for their happiness, whatever that looks like for them. They are relaxed with me and know I have no expectations that they do what I want for them. They are loved unconditionally. They are free, and so am I.

I ask myself, "Is there any benefit to me, or even for them, by sharing my thoughts on any given subject?" And if in doubt, this is when I ask myself, "Is it kind? Is it true? And is it even necessary?" If it's not all three, I don't say or do anything.

3. *Take What You Like, and Leave the Rest*

THIS IDEA REALLY gave me permission to use information that appealed to me. I tended to have black or white thinking twenty years ago. I had been raised by highly opinionated parents. Once I started questioning my beliefs to see if they were actually mine, and also whether I wanted them to begin with, I began entertaining new ideas that would work for me. I like the freedom and the notion that I don't have to accept anything that feels wrong to me. Also, I can try things out and give myself options. I don't have to figure out everything I do and every aspect of something before I try it.

I like feeling good about myself. I can love people and yet dislike their behaviors, or their bad habits. Once, I left the religion of my youth, and I was considering trying it again, but I was very cautious and suspicious about returning because I did not agree with many of the church's doctrines. I felt torn and restless, not wishing to be a perfectionist in my participation or lack of participation. I called this wonderful man that I'd met who was in the clergy, and I confessed my plight of not wanting to be a hypocrite. He smiled and reminded me to take what I like and leave the rest, which floored me at the time.

This was, and is, a revolutionary approach that I use today to identify exactly what I want to think and what I want to use when I lose an old, worn-out behavior or an old friend or an old lifestyle that's no longer working. My heart and my mind become more willing to risk defeat or rejection. I enjoy the journey and feel exhilarated by life's challenges. I also find I am less inclined to beat myself up if I decide on a different path or person. I like the flexibility and feel empowered. My spirit feels empowered instead of letting my perfectionism take me hostage. I allow myself the right to change my mind, and guess what? You have the right to change your mind. Being no longer imprisoned by what others think, or when I decide to play the geisha and start anticipating the needs of others, permits me the joyous luxury of knowing and honoring and loving myself. I allow myself to have and hold my very own preferences, satisfied and content. I then enjoy the opportunity to be happy and gracious when I decide to take what I like and leave the rest. I forgo shame and blame this way as well.

4. *We No Longer Pursue the Tormentor*

WE NO LONGER pursue the tormentor. If there is one idea that has impacted my actions and my attitude the most, it would be this one. When my mentor coach first said this to me over the phone, I asked her to repeat it three times. I was in shock as if hit by a taser or stun gun. When I talk in groups, I often find their responses are similar to mine. The clarity of how I brought so much pain into my life by pursuing tormentors was mind-blowing.

Tormentors are all-knowing, all-controlling, arrogant to the tenth degree, super demanding, and impossible to please. My tormentors brought me to my knees, and they always expect perfection. I had parents who demanded the best and never expressed their gratitude or praised me for anything. They needed me to be perfect. Not surprisingly, I attracted tormentors everywhere I went. I was driven by the insanity of needing love and approval from people who were incapable of expressing it. I sought love from sociopaths and narcissists. The more they withheld their love, the more I would push forward to get it.

When the tormentor decided to be snide or mean, I just hung out. I just hung around, thinking that eventually he would come to his senses and shower me with compliments and attention and love. I now realized for the first time that no one can give what they haven't got. This knowledge allowed me to stop pursuing relationships with self-obsessed people.

The other way I use this concept is to stop asking probing questions and expecting them to fulfill my needs and wants. Tormentors don't care about anyone's needs but their own. Tormentors need fans, adoring fans, or at the very least, members of their kingdom.

5.   *I Do an Adequate Job at a Moderate Pace*

THIS IDEA MUST look very beige and lacking in passion, but work-ing to exhaustion is pointless. Yet so many feel they must work hard and put their nose to the grindstone. Why? My health and serenity are much more precious than any amount of money. In my case, diagnosed with MS, it is essential to pace myself and not overdo my activities. I can almost hear some of you saying to your-selves, "Great, she's giving people permission to be lazy." The word "adequate" means "competent," or "enough," or "suitable," and my favorite definition is "fully sufficient." So where's the problem?

If I'm happily doing my job, and I'm accomplishing what I need in a fully sufficient way, there shouldn't be any reason to work any harder. Our world is overflowing with wounded people; the walking wounded often have to work to support themselves when they are clearly incapable of doing so. Many of us must work even harder to care for ourselves and the severely wounded and completely lost people. Nobody gets a truly free ride these days. If folks do live as a barnacle off someone else's back, they pay a heavy price with their self-worth. Does anyone know the names of the persons who carved Mount Rushmore, built the Eiffel Tower? Or how about the slaves who cut and hauled the stones of our Egyptian pyramids—anyone know who they were? We push ourselves and miss our lives, and all for a dollar. We can't take our money, power, fame, awards, treasures, or even our memories with us when we die.

Do an adequate job at a moderate pace. You are not a better person or more appreciated by working ten-hour days or pushing yourself. There are plenty of slackers and loafers, it's true, but what's that got to do with you?

Today, I will not compare, complain, or condemn. I will do an adequate job at a moderate pace to provide for my needs. Today, I will eat well, sleep well. I will think of others less fortunate than I am and offer my service to them, and I will go outside as often as possible and enjoy Mother Nature. I do these things so I can live until I die. We don't know how much time there is in the dash on our headstones. It's your life; it's your time. I dare you to enjoy it.

6. *What Other People Think of Me Is None of My Business*

WHAT A RELIEF to find and embrace this idea! I only wish I had been introduced to this concept in eighth grade.

I grew up faster and was a few inches taller than 90 percent of the girls and most of the boys in my class. It takes confidence to succeed in any endeavor, and knowing who you are and liking who you are is extremely essential for life. By finding self-acceptance in my own worth, I can navigate the ups and downs in life, and they do come.

Wanting approval from everyone is a true handicap, and I call this "giving away my power"—the power to set my value and how I compare or compete with others. Not everything in life needs to be a competition. There is a time and place for competition, of course, and its use as an entertainment. Feeling good about ourselves is the key to happiness and so much more for all of us. For some, life and death.

I don't volunteer to have my personality judged anymore. I avoid putting myself at the mercy of unkind, unhealthy people. In the past, I'd ask, "What do you think about me?" Never did I ever question or think that you weren't thinking about me, because you were thinking about yourself. Now, if I start reading an email, and it starts off, "Deborah, you suck," I stop reading it, and I delete it. My happiness is my work, and it's an inside job. No one cares about me as much as I do. This is helpful to know, also, to remind me that you need to take care of yourself, and it's not my job.

Taken further, my life is none of my business, either, nor is your life any of my business, so what is my business or purpose? My business is to be of service to my Higher Power and all mankind and myself. My traits of people-pleasing and approval-seeking have been replaced by seeking spiritual lessons and by taking care of myself.

There are so many controlling, unkind, and unscrupulous people whom I have come into contact with, I would be lost if I had not learned to build my own loving picture of myself. I would have been annihilated. Today, when I do have a reason to put myself around crazy or mean-spirited people, I affirm out loud to myself, "If they don't like me, it's because they don't really know me. I am not what I do or what I have or what I look like. I do the very best I can every day to think, behave, and look my best. If it works for me and causes no harm to others, I am a success."

7. *Today, I Will Not Criticize, Complain, or Condemn*

WHAT THIS PHRASE means on a day-to-day basis is occasionally a tough one for me, but this discipline has really helped me mature. I encourage you to practice this idea because it will leave you so much more time for enjoyment. Go ahead and try not complaining or criticizing or condemning for six hours, so you can see how hard it is.

The deceased husband of one of my clients had a very low-grade contempt for her, and she could feel it. She told me, "I hate the feeling of being judged and gossiped about," and so after he passed away, she wanted to eliminate this destructive, insidious habit she'd picked up from him. She began to endeavor not to allow herself the bad habit of condemning and criticizing and complaining. She told me that she'd actually had suspicions the last few years of their ten-year marriage that her husband was gossiping about her and her kids, and her suspicions were confirmed when he did pass away. Quite by accident, she'd found a letter he'd written to his sister and ex-wife, condemning her and her entire family. She tore it up, she said. "I want to live in joy and hold myself up to high standards, not because I'm better than anybody or I want to appear saintly—I simply don't have time to waste. The past is dead and I am moving on." I taught her how to practice positive thinking and daily praising of others and their accomplishments because she wanted to feel good and calm and happy and playful.

Contempt, criticism, and complaining makes me tense, and I scowl, and I get a sinus headache. Life isn't fun when I'm listing complaints, grumbling about what did and did not happen. Self-discipline is a lifelong pursuit, and my commitment fluctuates, depending on my awareness. Turning off unproductive thinking can be as easy as flipping the switch.

I'm sure I mentioned that my own parents were highly critical, especially of my brother. Criticizing and complaining and condemning are the luxury of most comics. The main ingredient, as a matter of fact. I find it hard to imagine Ricky Gervais or Don Rickles being able to perform without the ability to criticize. They wouldn't have any material left. Their pessimistic, caustic way of seeing things and the ability to puff up the worst of things works for their exaggerated, comedic efforts, but it doesn't work for most people. I don't want what they have in their heads in my mind. It's scary, and I'm sure that I'd be a nervous wreck if I ever had an occasion to interview one of them.

Twenty-four hours at a time, I look on the bright side of things, and have trained myself from labeling events as good or bad, pleasant or unpleasant, because either way they are temporary, and they will change. The saying "This too shall pass" is a great comfort in times of stress. Treating events in the neutral way also allows me a way to detach and feel less upset about what life has to dish up.

Worry is the misuse of my imagination. The more I focus on an idea, the more I give it power. It is my ego that wants to convince me that there is a problem. The mind's eye helps me to create the blueprint for my thinking and the actions I take on a daily basis. If I dwell on what terrible things can, or worse, will happen, often enough, it will manifest. I didn't know that I could control or stop my thoughts.

Over the last twenty-three years, I developed this awareness that I do have that power. It began when I refused to see myself in a wheelchair, as I had been advised to get a wheelchair and practice using it when I was diagnosed with MS. Instead, I envisioned myself dancing on the grass and at the beach. I asked my Higher Power to guide my thoughts and actions on a higher plane. I meditated and saw myself in the shower, washing off the MS disease. I imagined myself as a seven-year-old, wearing a pretty lavender dress, carrying a bucket of fluffy, marshmallow-like paste in one hand and a magic wand in the other. I was accompanied by my loving dog, Smoothie, who carried a second bucket of my frothy goo. We went to each hardened lesion in my brain, painted large globs of the marshmallow goo on each myelin sheath. I did this every night.

Throughout my practice, I have asked my clients to create the visions of hope and healing and manifestation, and meditate on them before they turn in at night, and again just before leaving their bed in the morning. I shared how to wash away worry and fear while showering. The more specific the visions, the better. I put my attention on the positive outcomes I want, and I see what I want to happen in living color, as if I were watching the movie as it comes about. I write my desires out. I write want ads for exactly the outcomes and qualities I desire. I wrote a "man wanted" ad with forty must-have items and characteristics and qualities and put it in my treasure box. One and a half years later, my current husband materialized with every trait but one, which was an either/or request. Just as an architect draws his plans, so do I envision and affirm the blessings I am ready to embrace.

When doom and fear present themselves in my mind, I follow that thought with one of the ideas in this book. Depression is self-obsession, and the antidote for me is service to others and more intense use of positive affirmations. I know from my personal and my clients' experience that I must be free of any substance use and/ or anything else, a behavior or addiction, in order to effectively choose these higher tools for living. This is not hard work, but it does require persistence.

My clients enjoy me as their advocate and cheerleader; support groups of like-minded people really help with consistent practice of the following ideas that will set you free. Not only do I need to fight off my demons and doubts, but also the fears and doubts and outright attacks from others. Many married couples and lovers can't truly support their partners in this way because they feel somehow impotent or, sadly, to blame for their partner's difficulties. Learning how to love and detach and support your partner requires deep self-love and emotional maturity. Learning how to live with personal disappointment, health challenges, financial challenges, and see them not as failings but growth opportunities is a lofty, yet attainable goal. A goal which, if supported by both partners holding an optimistic attitude, can truly forge an unbreakable union. When I envision the best outcome and take the time to clearly know what I need, there is less fear. There is less free-floating fear and anxiety.

I used to wake up feeling like I was already behind, already flawed. Once I started clarifying my desires, and even asking my Higher Power to work out solutions while I slept, my morning madness was replaced by intuitive thoughts, ideas, solutions, creative notions that flooded my mind upon awakening. I set the tone of my day before my feet hit the ground by asking my higher self how I can benefit my family and friends and clients. I no longer feel lost. I thank my Higher Power for the day and set about my morning absolutions.

8. *Turn Off the Sound and Watch the Picture*

LEARNING TO PROTECT yourself in business and matters of the heart is a must these days. Let's face it: Man, woman, young, old—we all have the ability to twist the truth to serve our selfish needs. By learning to protect ourselves, using our powers of observation, and waiting to see if actions match the words of any potential relationship, we can truly learn to take care of ourselves.

People-pleasing and ignoring red flags is a common mistake of love-hungry people of all ages. This is especially true when involved with alcoholics or addicts. Practicing their disease, or even not, these people believe what they say deeply when they say it, but once under the influence of their drug of choice, they lose all accountability.

However, the discerning have a much greater chance than those who simply listen with their hearts. It does take some time for people to let down their masks and show who they are and what their values and principles, and even their political and spiritual standards, are. Now, having said this, I know the flip side are the people who will keep everyone at arm's-length indefinitely. Well, I don't recommend this fear-based attitude at all. Life is not for the faint of heart, and risk-taking is needed if you want to find real joy.

I have also used this phrase—"Turn off the sound and watch the picture"—to assess results when it comes to business. Reading the fine print is often neglected in the excitement of buying something new or starting a new relationship. The first ninety days of any relationship can always be an opportunity to be swayed by false promises and idealistic talk. Watching the actions, and even journaling and keeping track of outcomes, has proven over and over to be extremely beneficial to me, and to those whom I have coached.

I ask myself why I do or don't do something. What is my motivation? Is it selfish, self-serving? Is it coming from my litany of fears? Well, if it is any of the above, it will not work out well. If I act for my integrity, self-worth, self-honesty, I will have a smooth, rewarding journey. It begins and ends with me honoring, knowing, and loving myself well.

9. *What You Resist, Persists*

BY INTERNALIZING THIS concept, you will be more willing to reach for acceptance. If you look back at several events in your past life, you will probably see that by resisting, you actually added more and more misery to your life. It's true for me, too. In 2005, my husband, son, and pets and I moved into an apartment building my parents owned in Santa Monica for what we thought would be a temporary, two-month stay.

Well, it turned into an eighteen-month stay because of various circumstances, including my mother breaking her hip. And I have to say that I was not a happy girl. We were tripping over each other and scooting between boxes, and I resisted and whined and complained until one day I remembered the phrase, "What I resist, persists." I had given this phrase to many clients over the years.

Finally, I knew what I had to do. I had to decorate the apartment. Make it cozy and tidy. I had to act as if I loved living there. Once I did that, the universe responded immediately, showing me all the conveniences and gifts I was receiving by being in this particular location. My mother's skilled nursing home was about ten minutes away, and I also had the best acupuncturist I had ever had just down the street from this particular building.

I began to see how this had all been an amazing blessing for me and my entire family. Not fighting what is opens the channel for what happens, and gratitude.

Nowadays, I make my plans loosely and watch what happens and remain as neutral as possible. I trust my intuitive thoughts and cast away all expectations. The next right thought and right action will be so evident.

For several of my clients, the results were similar. Acceptance doesn't always mean I agree with what is, or like what is. True, the most wonderful form of acceptance includes gratitude, which I usually get to when I reflect back on the incident a year or so later. But, nonetheless, non-resistance will do to unplug the bad energy so we can feel more comfortable.

I like to use what I call the Walter Cronkite approach to acceptance: "And that's the way it is."

One gentleman I coached was passed over by his firm for a younger man, who had only been with the company less than half a year. My client was counting on that promotion, and he was just furious to have to account to this new man—this new, young man—and he really resisted working with him, and he resisted my suggestion that he become willing to accept the new hierarchy at work. Well, after a while, my client decided to try it, and it became easier and easier over the next few weeks.

Then one day, the new man—the new department director— was gone. And my client found out that he'd been given this job, chosen, because he was so young, and he was flown overseas to start up a new branch, and they chose him because he was single and had no ties. My client was then given this particular job, the top position, and given twice his salary for pay, and all because he was willing to accept and stop resisting.

By going with the flow, or what's happening, I struggle less, and you'll struggle less, and you'll exercise your faith muscles. If something is scary or unclear, you can still relax and write a positive affirmation, or post a positive gratitude message to yourself on a whiteboard. By surrendering your demands and outcomes and trusting that all is well, you honor the universe. You honor the universal truths of living in the now. Then, and only then, does the energy shift and allow for change to occur. Now, this is true for me, and has been most true for every person that I've worked with who has stopped resisting what is.

10. *"No" Is a Complete Sentence*

WHY IS SAYING "no" so difficult for so many of us? I attribute it to fear of abandonment. Being raised by addicted or mentally ill or dysfunctional parents, or with sick or abusive siblings, sets us all up to be approval-seekers and people-pleasers. We will deny or minimize our wants, needs, and beliefs to gain or retain love, success, security, and have our financial and our sexual desires met.

Some of us, including me, were taught to be polite, or not make waves, and always submit to authority figures. One older woman who worked with me was a newlywed. She had married a retired businessman, a veteran, and sought me out for coaching. She wanted me to help her get her husband to change. He was an alcoholic and stayed at home watching porno, while she worked and paid the bills. He made greedy requests for use of her money and her car.

They separated, and she was doing great, learning how to say no firmly and calmly, but unfortunately, her fears of abandonment and of growing old alone got the better of her. Because she couldn't say no, she subjected herself to physical, financial, and emotional abuse. She had stopped working with me when she decided to take him back.

Another lady I coached with her dating and work issues with her assistants and her direct boss. This middle-aged lady was a real go-getter and had a joyous personality. She interacted with a lot of young and old people. Raised to be very proper, she often spread herself so thin, not wanting to disappoint, that she didn't have time for herself. Not knowing how to say no, and fearing disapproval, left her forever angry at herself, and also guilty. I explained that by saying yes when she meant to say no, she was really lying, and thereby abandoning herself and her own needs, and her light came on. We role-played until she felt secure. We book-ended her telephone calls when she began utilizing her right to say no.

Another handsome, older gentleman I coached has had a very difficult time saying no to his grown children, especially his son, the baby of the family. Through coaching with me, he began to understand that saying no was allowed, and often a blessing that could help his son take better care of himself.

Today, I never let people pester me to rush a decision. I tell pushy people, "If I have to decide this minute, the answer is no. Give me some time, and I'll consider it."

The idea that saying no without giving my reason or excuses seems odd to most of the clients whom I've coached. The good-girl or the nice-boy training from childhood leads many of us to believe that we have to have good manners at all times; therefore, we owe some explanation to those who have made a request. This idea isn't true, and we are accountable only to ourselves, and the few we choose to trust.

I simply say, "No, and thanks for thinking of me," or, "No, thank you, that won't work for me." They're both the only responses needed. I suggest to all whom I coach that they ask themselves why—why they would say yes. What is your motive for saying yes to any request? If you say yes because you are fearful, guilty, or feel obliged, or want to impress or rescue, then you are not taking care of yourself and are heading for disappointment and trouble. If you need to check and see what you have coming up in your calendar, that is perfectly understandable.

A dear, dying friend of mine said that if I am struggling to make a decision, it's usually the wrong decision. If I have mixed feelings or confusion about what feels right to me to do, I say no. I have learned to stand in my truth.

Just as I asked myself about saying yes, the same holds true for when I say no. Am I saying no out of fear? How about anger, or needing to control or manage someone or something? Is my motive clean and truthful, without attitude or arrogance? Am I trying to save, fix, or mother someone? Learning to speak your truth, whether it is going to be received with gratitude or not, gives each of us the integrity we need to fuel our own personal growth.

11. When I Take Care of Myself, I Give Everyone Else Permission to Do the Same

THERE IS ALWAYS a flip side to the truths I put forth to you, none more obvious than this one. The savages in our universe have no trouble taking care of themselves. So the above phrase is really geared to the more enlightened person—people who think of others and their needs before taking care of themselves. The givers want to give, and the takers will be happy to take, and take, and take as much as they can get. This idea, truth, is geared for all loving givers out there. The trouble for givers is that they feel guilty and selfish. The reality is, if you don't take care of yourself, who will? No one.

One of my clients in L.A. was the daughter of a famous, prolific writer. She was haughty and controlling—quite a character, as a matter of fact. She had everything one could wish for, materially, as she had been left a great inheritance. But because of her wealth, she treated people in a dismissive fashion. Her live-in boyfriend, Eric, was at least ten years younger. This lady, in her early fifties, did not take care of herself in business or in love. She was always dealing with angry exes and with lawyers, forever complaining everyone was trying to rip her off. It was only after several coaching sessions with me that she started seeing and owning her part in these recurring events. By not taking care of herself, and asking questions and putting herself first, she put herself at risk. She had lost a lot of money, and she'd lost a lot of self-respect.

After a very few months of utilizing the idea to take care herself first, she stopped feeling guilty about how much money she had and about how many things she had control over. She was empowered and could finally take risks only when in her comfort level, and for her highest, best interest.

The idea of taking care of yourself may seem contrary to what church-goers and good Samaritans believe. However, we each have one life, one body, one mind, one soul with which we must use wisely in this plane of existence. Just as we maintain our homes, our cars, and our careers, it makes sense to take care of ourselves. To quote the promises of the AA Big Book of Alcoholics Anonymous, "We cannot give something we haven't got." We must take care of ourselves first to be fit spiritually to give out of our abundance.

My client stopped treating people in a self-superior way. She became loving and grateful for her good fortune, and generous to her family and friends. Lots of hurting people are trying to grab as many material possessions as possible to show their worth and feel abundant. One trip to the skilled nursing facility will show you just how empty that is as a life pursuit.

Today, I take care of myself physically, emotionally, financially, and spiritually. And as a result of my continuous practices of self-reflection, positive thinking, self-acceptance, and alignment of my willpowers with God's will, I am living heaven on earth. No longer a slave to my lowest instincts and ego, I soar above the day-to-day struggles of living in an abrasive world.

12. I No Longer Take My Toys to People Who Will Break Them

IN MY EARLY thirties, a darling senior lady taught me this idea. I had the bad habit of giving up too much personal information to people—mostly men I barely knew. My nerves would get the better of me, especially when out on a date with someone new. I have since suggested this notion to several people I have worked with.

One beautiful lady in her forties that I knew in show business was unable to stop talking. She could not be still if someone was present to listen. She would talk quickly and she was quite funny and clever. Even though she did get teased about her constant chattering, her personality was adorable. And she was well liked. She was quite charming and pretty, but had real trouble being comfortable on dates because she'd divulge too much information and feel silly and vulnerable. She had a fear of silence. It was a challenge to help her find and hold on to her sense of worth.

After eight months of discussion, she had an awakening that she didn't have to perform all the time. With guided meditation and simple quiet time, she embraced the idea of protecting herself by not giving away secrets and beliefs. Her dating became much more pleasant for her, and she met a dear man whom she's been happy with for several years now.

Learning to research companies, prospective tenants, and cross-check references is an absolute must nowadays. When I take my toys to people who will break them, it's because I'm too lazy to investigate who I'm dealing with, their values, and what exactly they stand for. When falling for a new person, it is best not to give too many details about my life, where I work, what I need to be happy. My creative projects have to be in a safe environment to blossom. I, too, had to learn the hard way by having clothing ruined and by having loaned items damaged or lost. I don't lend money, clothes, or cars, or share intellectual ideas with people I don't trust.

13. I Speak My Truth Once, and Either They Get It, or I Get It—Get It?

I REALLY WAS mystified when my coach told me this idea. I was a very stubborn child, and my nickname was, "She's Mighty Determined," and I certainly had to let you know how and when you hurt me. I would give you one example after another so you really, really understood the terrible, bad things you did to me. And then, if I perceived any trouble, and I had any fear about something that might happen, I had to warn you, didn't I?

Sadly, I was like a broken machine stuck in a fear-control groove. This notion of saying my truth once and only once seemed highly suspect, and unlikely to work. Many times, I've said my truth, and I can see by the recipient's expression and response that they do not, in fact, understand me. And no amount of repeating my explanation can cut through their fog. This was a huge revelation to me—the idea that some people wouldn't "get me."

When I realized that no amount of people-pleasing could make some folks like me, or want me, or want what I had, well, I finally got it. We are all different. We don't all think the same.

One lovely client of mine named Vicky—she's a stay-at-home mother of two very young sons—has had a very difficult time believing in speaking her truth with her parents. Since her abusive and addicted parents say inappropriate things in front of their grandchildren, and say critical and vulgar things to my client, I recommended that she have little contact because she'd had several disappointing conversations. And it took a long time, but she finally got that her parents are toxic, and without treatment, will remain that way. The belief that "this time" they will be different has taken her several months to finally let sink in. My client had been attempting to show them the error of their ways since her childhood. And on the days Vicky accepts that her parents are ill, she has peace and serenity, and her life really works. And on the days that she forgets, she's in chaos.

Another young man, Jerry, a physical therapist whom I coached, had a very contentious relationship with his coworker, Max. Jerry's boss was oblivious to the shenanigans that Max would pull on Jerry during treatment sessions in front of the clients. Jerry was sheepish about making waves, and made hollow threats and weak requests for Max to "grow up." After coaching with me, he was able to say directly and calmly that he would report Max to the boss the next time he pulled a prank. Jerry said his truth once, and Max just laughed it off. So Jerry went to the boss, who was equally unprofessional, and in essence told Jerry to just suck it up. After a coaching session with me, Jerry then realized that he had, in essence, recreated his family role with his relationship with his older brother and his dismissive father. Jerry then decided to quit that job and work elsewhere. It took him only a month to find a great job at twice the salary.

14. I Don't "Should" on You, Please Don't "Should" on Me

IT IS AMAZING how habitual it has become to use the word "should" in our society. "You should try this restaurant." "You should try this haircut." "You should try this food." All the things we decide we enjoy or that we like to do, we feel we have to pass on to someone else. But none of us knows what is right for someone else. When I stopped saying the word "should" in my conversations, it felt very odd at first, probably because it is so commonly used. Perhaps we feel closer to someone if they follow our advice. Maybe we "should" people because we have nothing else to say.

There is a pushy vibe when I tell you, "You should not eat candy," or, "You should not drink that." If you are at all like me, if you tell me you should do this or that, I will do the exact opposite, or nothing. Nowadays, if I get "should" on, I thank the person for their suggestion and leave it at that.

This saying came to me while I was coaching a sixteen-year-old girl. Randy was still living at home with abusive, alcoholic parents, who were alternately permissive and controlling. I found Randy saying on more than one occasion that her mother said she should do this and she should do that so often that Randy felt constantly behind schedule and inherently flawed all the time.

As is often the case with out-of-control drinkers, there were many occasions that Randy was unsupervised, and she took full advantage of staying out late at night, and she ultimately got pregnant. I coached Randy to tell her parents everything, and to use the phrase, "I don't should on you; please don't should on me." She was able then to express to her parents her fears about their drinking, and ask them to seek help.

Mom and Dad were amazingly open to what she was sharing; well, they were shocked, and initially full of guilt and shame for having let this all happen. But a shift took place for all of them. They sought recovery and helped Randy with her pregnancy and were very supportive.

15. *Rejection Is God's Protection*

WHEN I DON'T get what I want, instead of feeling sorry for myself or angry, I remind myself of this concept. Whatever I attach my mind to becomes an expectation, which may or may not materialize. By cultivating a relationship with my Higher Power or God of my own understanding, I surrender outcomes. I do all the footwork, and God does all the worrying. Hindsight has always been my friend, because when I am honest with myself, most of my wants are simply self-serving. Defeated or rejected, I can see how I always benefit when I think of the good of all instead of just myself and what I think will be good for me. This is proven true the majority of the time.

After considerable soul-searching, I became aware that many of the things that I believed I must have in order to be happy were not my ideas at all. They were someone else's, or society's, or the government's, or a system of thought from old customs that bore no real meaning in today's culture. My attitudes and desires were not chosen by me; they were hand-me-downs. I have seen the proof that what I do get in this life is my choice, if I see it as such. I am no longer a leaf, blowing here and there. I decided there is only one of us here, and there is plenty for all of us.

Rejection takes me out of harm's way and sets me back on track. Instead of trying to make things happen, I co-partner with my Higher Power to do and say what is best for us all. My mindset is my own design these days.

Rejection protects me from my ego's insatiable desire for more, and more, and more. Rejection allows me to let go and trust what is. To the extent that I resist what is, I suffer. I do footwork, lots and lots of footwork, putting myself out there, risking everything, knowing that whatever I do, I am a winner just for making my attempts.

Rejection keeps me from throwing more rocks into my canoe. It cuts the weight free, and I flow more freely down the stream of life. I waste less time and energy chasing what isn't mine. By knowing rejection is God's protection, I am more serene more of the time. I am more ready to find what is better for me. I seek my own approval first. I become my own white night. I keep my pearls to share with my true love. All love is useful, and never wasted, even if it's not reciprocated. Nothing is permanent. People change, move away, die, and I must relinquish control, or be dragged. Timing and positioning are key to my alignment, but nothing is stagnant if it is to remain alive. Selecting an attitude that serves me is my decision.

16. People Don't Do Things to Me. They Do and Act for Themselves, Without Thinking About Me

THIS NOTION REMOVES my need to blame, and any tendencies I may have to play the victim. Greed, fear, lust, and control are the traits that motivate the vast majority of people on this earth, especially when societies are forever teaching us to compete and compare and to conquer each other. And for what? We will all die, and won't be able to take anything with us. Each of us has roughly twenty years from twenty to forty to make our fortunes and create our families. We spend between eight to twenty years preparing and studying so that we'll have the skills we need to succeed at our careers. And then we spend another eight to twenty years protecting and managing our spoils so we can leave them to our families.

When people thwart our efforts or steal our treasures, we have a tendency to spend our thoughts on revenge and restitution. We forfeit our most precious, non-recoupable asset—time. Time, which when spent, is gone, never to be returned.

I had several financial challenges that I inherited when my mother passed away. Three different groups of people finagled large sums of money from her properties. They were all motivated by fear and greed. Because I've adopted the idea that they are spiritually sick and acting out of their defects, I can pray for them and forgive them, because they are sick and will continue to suffer until they work towards changing. So it's a complete waste of my life to be jealous, angry, worried, guilty, or afraid. If taken to heart and internalized, the ideas in this book will be your recipe for a peaceful, joyous, exciting life.

17. *I Do Not Audition for Love*

GROWING UP AS I did, like so many of us, in a dysfunctional family, made me an approval-seeking missile. My worth as a woman was in the hands of every person I met. The opposite sex, especially, was the arbiter of my value as a woman. My father nicknamed me "the golden stripper" for some unknown reason. My mother allowed no displays of affection and pushed my father aside whenever he tried to hug her or kiss her. So the message was to objectify myself and to have delivery of a child by immaculate conception. Please look at me, but don't touch me, was a very confusing message for a teenage girl.

After two marriages, I understood that I was dating and committing to men for the wrong reasons with the wrong motives and a lousy sense of worth. An eighty-three-year-old woman, Margaret, told me I was lovable just because. She said I was God's princess, and she told me she was his queen.

I started affirming that I am the gem, I'm the jewel, I'm the prize, I'm the party. And at first it felt silly saying that out loud. I am completely convinced today that I am all that and more. Today, I am married to the love of my life. My third husband died suddenly in 2007 at the age of sixty. I began dating on online dating services two years after he passed away. I wrote a "man wanted" ad to the universe on a yellow legal pad with all of the qualities and assets my ideal man would need to possess. And please remember, I was fifty-six at that time, and I also had multiple sclerosis. I was patient for eighteen months of dating. After dating several men, I found my darling husband in 2010, and we were wed this past May of 2012. He has everything on that list, everything I put on my list of wants.

When dating, I had an attitude of being on a fact-finding adventure. I was looking for a person to invest my time with. Even if the man wasn't "the one," I could at least have a new friend. I did not go on a date hoping I was good enough. I know I am good enough, and that everyone who knows me has to like me, and if they don't, it's because they don't really know me.

I do not audition for love because I love myself, and that is extremely attractive to everyone I meet. I have coached many women with this system of dating to see if someone has what they want. Instead of thinking I can change a man to suit me, I observe who they are for a few months without sex. I am easily bonded to a man once I experience sexual intimacy. Heavy petting and oral sex are equally vulnerable for many woman, and I suggest waiting a few months for that as well.

One client, a stunning forty-year-old lady with two young daughters, was very grateful to work with me. Sunny was her name, and she was awkward on dates and felt obliged to "perform" at least oral sex, even on a first date. I confided in her my story of the Jacuzzi man who morphed into the farting man. This story typified my extreme case of people-pleasing, a trait I acquired from being raised to always be polite, and how I finally got over that insane behavior. This is a funny and sad story I share only with my clients.

18. Nothing Changes Until Something Changes, and Nothing Ever Changes Until It Gets Too Painful to Stay the Way It Is

ALAS, THIS IS human nature. That said, you'd be amazed how many people enjoy whining and "pewling"—that's a Texas saying—insisting that they, whoever they are, need to change. I ask my clients to tell me straight up, "Are you part of the problem, or are you part of the solution?" This always feels like a board between the eyes. Then I ask, "Which do you want to be?"

Even if I am the "victim," I am guilty of doing the tormentor a spiritual disservice by permitting or volunteering for the abuse or injustice. To be spiritually fit, I must stand up for myself. If I don't, my inner child will surely have a temper tantrum, and I will not rest until I do stand up, or numb myself with one of my drugs of choice.

There is nothing attractive about playing the martyr. Submission is out of style in most larger cities in the USA, I like to think. A trip to Brazil or Costa Rica is the target location for the men who long for the old days when women were chattel. Fortunately, my mother did give me one glorious message, that I was equal to all people, including any man. I love men, and being an equal doesn't mean I can't be feminine. I enjoy being a girl, and highly recommend it to the women I coach.

So since I can't change anybody but myself, what do I change? Well, I can change my actions and my attitudes. I challenge my clients to figure this out. All of us hold all of the answers we need for change. I find my answers by writing to my Higher Power. I have a Goddess of my understanding. I read my letters to a trusted coach or mentor. I find it is too uncomfortable to share my process with family and friends. Family and friends may love me, but they often lack the detachment needed to let me sort things out the way I can with a mentor. Some may be able to speak with clergy or ministers or a superior at work. For me, I must first decide that I want to change, and then I must act in accordance with that decision.

Here's an example. Simon wanted to quit smoking. He had tried several times. I explained that wanting to quit and deciding to quit were not the same. Deciding to quit and doing the actions, or not doing the actions, that fulfill that decision, is how things change. Simon decided not to buy or bum any cigarettes each morning, and he no longer smokes, and hasn't for twelve years now. He also laughed and told me that he decided that if one cigarette flew into his mouth, he'd smoke it. If a craving hit him, I told him it would pass even if it wasn't satisfied. I suggested drinking lots of water and eating fruit for the first ten days.

An older woman, Constance, came to me complaining of her abusive husband. He drank too much and didn't work and watched porno, she suspected. We met for three months. She made progress, but ultimately let her fear of being alone in her advanced years get the better of her. She had described a time when he left her in a bad neighborhood. He actually took off, driving her car. He demanded she give him her paycheck. She even got as far as moving out from "her apartment" and staying with friends. And he hit her, stole from her, cheated on her. He had several girlfriends on Facebook. She gave up on our coaching and went back to him. She had not reached her bottom when it came to her pain.

I included this story for any of you still living in fantasy land. You can't drag a dead horse up a hill. Let go. Keep climbing. There is a new world waiting on the summit.

19. *People, All People, Are Self-Justifying*

REGARDLESS OF WHO you are, how you were raised, what you know, what you do for work or your career, who you know, where you live, etc., we all form prejudices and find ways to justify our choices so we can validate and support our opinions.

The book *Mistakes Were Made, but Not By Me*, written by Carol Tavris and Elliot Aronson, goes into the details and the reasons why the above statement is true. By gifting small items, companies, governments, and individuals can set up in us an indebtedness which, in turn, allows us over time to be swayed into behaving as the givers, and their vested interests, would want us.

I mention all this because some of you may want to keep consistent with your core beliefs, and to go a step further, to actually take a good, long look at your current beliefs. Challenging yourself in this way often produces huge personal breakthroughs.

Self-reflection, done in a daily, monthly, and yearly system, will help you truly attain self-mastery and enhance your life process. I promise. This will help you live in alignment with your personal standards.

When I acknowledged and accepted that my standards are mine, not yours, I became more than halfway to peace of mind. Now, I understand that everybody has finely honed biases, and I am given the gift of humility and, far more importantly, the tolerance needed to live my life free of worry and the need to control, fix, rescue my children, parents, siblings, mates, and friends, and even my so-called foes—foes who have decided to do things their way and are basically amateurs practicing my own personal defects of thought and behaviors. That's pretty crazy, right? Yet, that is what we do, many of us, do on a daily basis. This separation of me against them, or we, our tribe, against them. I, me, against you, or we, us, against "them." We suffer the more we demand our own personal positions.

It is impossible to avoid toxic people. People driven by fear and greed have blinders on. They spend their time in a constant state of wanting more of their share, and are rarely satisfied. Some spend 90 percent of their lifespan in acquisition mode and use the last 10 percent to be rid of it. Oh, well. Not my idea for fulfillment.

Knowing that that is the paradigm for the majority of people on this planet is seductive. It makes you want to join the race, or the opposite, to say "the hell with it" and live in scarcity. I want to be neutral, in essence, believing as I do that I was born into abundance and I have a right to it. Yes, even a duty to use all my gifts and blessings and ideas so they live on after I die.

What I coach is how to be happy and complete, no matter what life throws my way. No matter what anybody does, says, or doesn't do or say. My happiness is an inside job, and I have no right to spew my fear and worry and negativity on anybody else. This is a high standard, and I hold myself up to it because I like how my life looks and how I feel. Knowing that we all can find ways to be unconscious and numb out or deceive ourselves doesn't much help me to deal with its realities.

My programs and this book are my first-aid kit to survive the slings and arrows thrown by the savage, abrasive personalities that I will inevitably meet on the highway of life.

20. *They Have the Right To Be Wrong*

THEY HAVE THE right to be wrong. I apply this idea to people who are engaging in what I consider harmful habits, such as using illegal drugs or drinking or stealing. It also helps me to get along with people whom I disagree with. Now, to be clear, I'm not saying people have the right to do harm to others in any way. I feel people that kill, maim, or abuse others are sick people and should be separated and kept away from civil, loving, productive people at the very minimum. No, when I'm speaking about having the right to be wrong, it could be that I'm in a group and I disagree with policies or practices. I don't have to allow myself to personalize our differences this way. I can always find another group to join, or I can change my attitude, if it's not a big issue for me, and I know that by asking myself, "Is this really important?"

"They have the right to be wrong" is a comforting reminder, also, when I'm trying or I'm tempted, let's say, to manage or direct somebody else.

I speak my truth once, and either they get it, or I "get it," get it? I have a duty to myself to speak up and share my feelings and thoughts. Especially for the sake of authenticity in an intimate relationship, I must always voice my concerns openly. But repeating and trying to force my ideas on others is abusive and controlling and nagging. Once is enough, when I speak my truth. No more is needed.

Turn off the sound and watch the picture. People often say things and even believe what they are saying when they're asserting it at the time. It is the actions we take that truly show what people believe. If what I see does not reflect the promise that you made, I now must decide what is my best course of action. No shame or blame or reminding will help. No, I must take care of myself, whatever that looks like.

21. *Identify Instead of Criticizing or Comparing or Competing*

WHAT DO I mean when I speak of identification? It is the process of compassionate, deep listening and sharing my personal feelings and thoughts with a loved one or anyone else I wish to be kind to. I share my personal experiences, if appropriate, with the trouble source. By appropriate, I mean if what I wish to say feels safe for me and helpful and encouraging to them.

I feel people tend to love me and like me because I'm human and mess things up and make mistakes, not in spite of that. Identification is loving and forgiving and empowers us all. Identification with others' circumstances and difficulties allows the other person to relax and fire their on-call defense attorney that their ego has continuously retained. Yes, this attorney is ready to lay out all the excuses and justifications he can muster to protect the ego. Identifying goes beyond all the shame and the fears we all face daily. When I identify with kindness and my truth, I lift people up and inspire courage and self-worth for my fellows.

I was at a spiritual retreat in Palos Verdes and that's when I first learned, or I became introduced and encouraged to try identifying with my own children and my husband at the time, and it worked so well I decided to start suggesting it to clients. So I began with the father I was working with. George was his name. He'd come to me at his wit's end. Newly divorced, George and his only son, Sloan, were completely at odds. George had been unhappily married for nineteen years, and like many unfulfilled married men, he had made his work his escape from a woman, his wife,

Mindy, whom he could hardly stand to be in the same room with. So he had hid himself in his Century City office, and therefore was a completely absent father to his only son, Sloan.

Now that his son Sloan was seventeen, George had finally freed himself from his self-imposed prison and gotten the divorce he wanted. George had had an awakening during his divorce and really wanted to be the father he'd always wanted to be. But the trouble now was that Sloan didn't even care what his parents were up to anymore. He'd stopped hoping for a real family experience by the age of fourteen. George's newfound emancipation had made him really eager to be part of his son's life. He wanted to bond, even have Sloan live with him, if possible. Predictably, Sloan was not keen about this newfound attention from his dad, George. No, George was spooning it out pretty heavily. They were virtually strangers stepping into a whole new world.

George and I coached several months on his communication skills. He told me the single best tool he took away from our sessions was this idea of identifying with Sloan instead of trying to teach, guide, or control him. In Sloan's second-to-last semester in high school, he did very poorly and came home with a couple of D's and a fail on his report card. George explained that he employed the identification technique and shared some of his poor grades and experiences, and instead of shaming and punishing Sloan, had hugged his son and encouraged him and told him he was confident that Sloan, his son, had the smarts and pride to figure out how to improve his grades. George even offered to be of help by helping him study or getting him a tutor if he wanted one.

George told me a few months later that Sloan succeeded in his final semester, and that the conversation about the poor grades and his identification thing was the bridge that opened the door to Sloan and his father's relationship.

Parents are often so afraid that their child's future is damaged that they scold and punish instead of trying to understand their kids, their kids' world, and all the pressures that are heaped on them by school, society, and often their mean-spirited peers. Identification is such a good way to communicate as an equal. It melts all defensiveness.

Another application of this was when I was coaching a young performer. Tammy, a gorgeous redhead, formerly from Indiana, had come to me to gain confidence when she was performing as a singer. Tammy was one of those wannabes that we see on Idol or The Voice. She was always singing at open mics and showcases all over L.A., Palm Springs, and sometimes in San Francisco. She told me it was a very nerve-wracking process, and she mentioned just out of the blue one day, "You know, everybody tries to outperform each other and be better than everyone else." She said, "I do it, too, and it makes me inhibited, and I find myself disgusted with myself and discouraged."

I suggested to her, "Why don't you try to see these singing opportunities differently? Instead of comparing and competing, try identifying with each singer as wanting to be their very best, the best that they can be? That nobody can be better than they are at being them, and no one can be a better Tammy than you are." She thought about this for a while, and then we talked about approaching performing as a whole as a form of service. Again, Tammy was able to shift out of fear and despair by using identification and the idea of performing as a means of service, and it became the root of her new paradigm.

Compare and despair, or identify and share your gifts. Well, this concept had changed everything, she said. Her confidence soared, and she was unstoppable. Tammy really began having fun doing what she loved to do when she'd perform with this new-found approach. She told me she was thrilled with our coaching.

She even was able to show up for auditions with the attitude that she'd come to know of being of service to her interviewers. She proclaimed to me with great joy, if it was to be her gig, nobody else would take it from her. And if it wasn't hers, nothing she could do would make it hers. She no longer was a slave to what other people thought of her. She knew who she was, and she was happy, and the outcomes of her auditions and singing appearances, and even reviews she got, really didn't define her anymore. And certainly, any rejection she faced did not define her talent.

One footnote I wish to include here is that by identifying with what other people are doing or going through or feeling does not mean playing the "can you top this" game. There are people who feel they have to be experts in everything. Not only be the expert, but let everyone they meet know how proficient they are at everything. I have three such people that leap to mind with this maddening habit of being able to know everything about everything, as well as be able to do everything, from building a house to singing arias to playing pro tennis or being a gourmet cook, train dogs, paint like Picasso, you name it, and by golly, they're experts. These folks are particularly difficult to have as a caregiver like a nanny, or some of my lovers, manicurists, or any ongoing service providers, because you just can't get away from them. This is not what I mean when I say identify with people. In these cases, I usually just praise these jack-of-all-trades and quietly escape from them. No, the idea is to commiserate with people's feelings and not see who's done more, etc., or try to best each other. This need to go one better than your fellows is a fairly common experience with young wives and their mothers-in-law. Oh, and also with men, you know, young and old, with their athletic abilities. "When I, in my day, I ran three miles in the snow to get to school, blah, blah, blah." No, we're talking about compassion in a nonjudgmental and understanding manner, not, "Can I top that!"

22. *I Have All the Time I Need*

ONE OF THE most important and most rewarding things that my spiritual journey has revealed over the years is that I have all the time I need. I do not need to push or stress in life to live up to some imaginary potential. I see people rushing through their lives attached to cell phones and iPads, and they are missing their lives.

We all have all the time we need. I also know that I need not waste one minute of this glorious life on earth with negative thinking or destructive actions or abusive people. I've decided each day to live moment to moment. I reference the past as I would when I would be driving a car, checking the rearview mirror occasionally to see where I'm coming from. I am mindful of the future and plan for it about six months ahead. I see many people obsessing and writing business plans and making goals, but are they going to be any happier when they get there? I doubt it.

Life is a series of choices, and I want love and joy as the main ingredients from the second my eyes open each morning until they close at night. I thought money and fame and adventure would fill me up. They are only fleeting, and nothing is mine to keep in this lifetime. The increasing pursuit of each and every obsession is the real culprit robbing us of our very life force and true purpose. I wish I had had the teachers and coaches and mentors I've had these twenty-plus years while I was still in grade school. That would've been great! The things I share in this book have given me and many people I've worked with better lives—happier lives. Life is what you think about, and then what you do about what you think.

A great friend of mine and my family, says, "Why do people have fear? Because they think thoughts that scare them. Hmm." Simple, yes? The self-imposed task-mastering in an inner critic, a needy, greedy voice, is my ego. I call mine "Shirley Temptress"— my ego, that is. I chose that because I spent my childhood and the years following into my late twenties trying to tap dance into the hearts of America, just like Shirley Temple Black did. During this period, I also tried to emulate Twiggy, Hayley Mills, Farrah Fawcett, Bridget Bardot, Doris Day, singer Blondie, and of course, Marilyn Monroe. It has been such a relief to find myself and like who I've found—a lady who is glad to be alive and able to love and help others.

I saw a post on Facebook from one of my grown twin sons today where he said exactly what I have come to believe—that Time is an illusion…manmade. That we live in the Now, and as it happens that is where God is…in the Now. There is no other time but Now. I therefore am always on time and where I need to be. I have exactly what I need right now and I will have exactly what I need forever.

It became so easy to be kind to myself and others once I changed from pursuing material possessions and needing to compete in all areas of my life, and simply falling in love with myself and my fellows.

23. *When I Am Doing More for Someone, Especially Addicts or Alcoholics, Than They Are Doing for Themselves, I Have Crossed the Line*

MOTHERS AND FATHERS and spouses and siblings and friends and lovers across the globe have a desperate need to help save, fix, the one they love so deeply. Because of this compulsive need to help, it's somewhat of a challenge, as their coach, to help them realize that when they do more for the person who is lost or in trouble or alone, they are doing the person a spiritual disservice.

If I go into hero mode and rescue or bail someone out of their consequences, I am cosigning the sufferer's low self-esteem and agreeing with them that they don't have what it takes to live successfully. Now, of course, a parent has a legal obligation to protect, provide a place to live, clothes to wear, and education, food, and medical attention for their child until they reach age twenty-one. Once the child is grown up, the parents are no longer on the hook, and their "help" can actually hinder or contribute to their child's problems.

Not only do I do the person a spiritual disservice, but by cosigning their low self-esteem, I am hurting myself. I'm harming myself by not tending to my own garden.

The most dramatic example I ever came across in my practice was when I coached a very unusual Russian girl, Natalia. She was uniquely lovely. She had pale skin and dark, shoulder-length hair, dressed very plainly, and used no makeup. She was almost ghost-like. I met her at the Director's Guild in Hollywood at a SAG screening. Natalia was very interested in film noir, and we struck up a conversation. After a while, she decided to have me coach her. After six months into our work, she explained that she'd had a pattern of getting involved with young men who were very ill, either physically or mentally. She then confided in me her deepest, darkest secret. She and her brother, her younger brother, had witnessed their father in his violent assault and bludgeoning of their mother when they were only eight and four. She and her brother were then sent to live with different extended family members, where she was then molested. She did not go into the details of what happened with her father and whether he was ever held accountable, but I got the impression that she didn't want to talk about it. She carried horrific guilt that she hadn't been able to save her mother. She'd been working for years on her dissertation, which she had decided to do on Hitler, of all things, and until she was coaching with me, she was completely unaware of the connection of her fascination with monsters. She had had an "aha" moment that Hitler and her father were one and the same—unfeeling and cruel.

Then Natalia was explaining that she had a pattern of being involved with several troubled men over the years. The most recent she was still in and had already been for three years. She had feared leaving him because he continued to threaten suicide if she ever left him. I referred her to a therapist at this point and helped her to give up her guilt of not being able to save her mother and helped her to forgive herself. She carried this guilt through childhood and had the shame of not being able to help her mother. She finally, through therapy, was able to forgive herself, and also to let go of the shame and the blame and put it where it truly belonged—on her terrible father.

Taking care of wounded men, she could distract herself from looking at this horrific childhood and keep trying to save someone she loved. Checking our motives and looking at the past is most productive whenever we feel uncomfortable. However, it is often overlooked. The day-to-day demands of living overshadow our thinking and overshadow taking stock of our lives and taking time to heal. Self-reflection pays off, though, especially if it's assisted by feedback from safe and knowledgeable professionals.

Women especially feel that their ultimate worth is based on having a man want them and gaining his stamp of approval. Another client, Missy, loved her husband so much. Everyone told her what a cute couple they made. Slim and fit, Missy was working her way up the ladder in her company while her husband stayed home watching TV and drinking beers. He was going to be a producer of films. Steven was also obsessed with golf and took himself to the golf course at least two times a week. However, he did nothing for his career.

Steven and Missy had been married just two years. She sought me out because I coached her best friend. When I asked her if she planned on having a family, it was as if the sky had opened up and the voice of God was speaking to her. She said, "Oh my God. I can't let him drive the children if he's a drunk." We had talked about how she was enabling him and cosigning his low self-esteem, but none of that penetrated her foggy thinking until I asked her about starting a family. That was the key—it was all right for her to live with a drunk but unacceptable for any of her unborn children. She would protect them before they were even here. Since then, when I speak to a woman who is being abused physically or mentally by her partner, I always ask if her daughter was being treated like that by an abusive partner, would it be okay? It always hits the maternal button of mother lioness defending her cubs. I remind these ladies they have an inner little girl, too, and she needs her protection desperately.

24. I Am No Longer Allowed to Hold Anyone Up to My Standards

THIS IDEA WAS given to me by a wise lady, Katy in West Covina. I was very concerned by my husband's behaviors and was willing to go anywhere for help. I remembered her talk a month or two earlier in Santa Monica and decided to seek Katy's advice.

Katy was very matter-of-fact in nature and laid her truth out without hesitation. This was the sentence she uttered that changed my life and saved my marriage: "I Am No Longer Allowed to Hold Anyone Up to My Standards." She told me this phrase applies to everyone, including spouses, parents, children, friends, religions, institutions, countries, employers, employees, businesses, service providers, the whole lot. It was a hard slap in the face. Sound preposterous? It's not.

There is a vast difference between employing discernment, exercising your personal preferences, and judging others according to your standards and the lens of your limited life experiences. The more I know who I truly am and exactly what my preferences are and what I need to live comfortably and honestly and feel safe and secure, the better my life feels to me. I can then take actions that will support my desires. Rather than setting the stage for disappointment with expectations of others by insisting that people do and say as I would have them, I have learned the only sure thing to count on is God, as I have come to know and trust Him.

Holding a person in contempt is a really arrogant and mean-spirited way to engage with another, even if you think it is subtle and they don't notice it. They do.

It is awful to roll your eyes, shrug your shoulders, turn your back, slam the door, stomp off out of the room. It is the ultimate put–down, eclipsed only by sheer indifference. But we pay with our soul when we descend into such stupidity.

Where do we get the idea that we know better than someone else? What gives us the right to set someone else's standards?

How can we be so belligerent and misguided when we know we all come from different cultures and that each generation predictably wants to shake up the status quo? Our children differentiate from us by adopting their own traditions, trends, and creative endeavors. They even use a new language and wear new styles to be unique in their age group.

How proud we are of our offspring until we start comparing their ways and wants with our own—then the struggle ensues. So many of us lack vision and come from fear trying to steer them to follow our plans. Don't they see we just want to "help them"?

Stanley was a businessman I coached to strategize growing his company, but after a few months, I could tell from his voice he was distressed, so I asked him what was up. "Stan," I said, "what's going on?" "It's my oldest son…he is such a disappointment. All he talks about is being an artist, and we have been over this a hundred times. I have been planning on him taking over my business since he was a junior in high school."

"Whoa," I said. "Stan, what makes you think it's okay to rain on your son's parade?"

He was silent for quite a while, then he said, "I don't know, I guess I always thought he'd take my place." After a minute or two, I shared this phrase with him: We are no longer allowed to hold anyone up to our standards.

He got a bit emotional and his voice broke slightly and he said, "You know, that sounds right. We are completely different people. I want him to follow his dreams, but I guess I worry he won't make any money at it. I don't know anything about the art world." He paused again. "I guess that is his right to take the risk. He might fail or succeed, and he'll have to figure out what's next. Just like I had to do."

When I do accept people as they are, it does not mean I have to agree with what they say or do or even with how they feel or think. As I allow others to do their "thing," I give myself permission to do mine.

Say you are married or living together, and the honeymoon phase is over, and both partners have made a mess of things. You now wonder if you have made a horrible mistake. Or perhaps you have a harmonious union most of the time, but once in a while, one or both of you lose it. Raging and yelling out ultimatums will not make things better, and you know it. Where do you go from here?

Look at the phrase again. You may not hold anyone else up to your standards. More often than not, that is the main problem. You cannot force your partner to acknowledge their part because you have no control over them. Go back and see what you thought you signed up for. Maybe you hadn't even considered whom this person was you were sleeping with. Maybe you don't know who you are and never considered asking yourself about that before you moved forward with this partner. It's not too late. Take some time and write about it, and get some clarity about your motives and expectations. Your partner may not want to do this process, and that's okay.

One of the best things I ever did for myself was to write out my definition of love. I found this so valuable I have shared this technique with several clients. It is very worthwhile to do. They all thank me. Some of my younger clients found this a bit challenging and even somewhat confusing. Turns out many of us think that love means I will do this and I will love you if you do that. This describes a conditional arrangement. Tit for tat is not love at all; it is barter.

Yet, many women I have coached have admitted that once they got married, they were now a unit, and so this fact had given them permission to expect to have some control over their husband's actions. After all, he was her husband!

I have to say that this attitude and belief is the single most common reason husbands and wives fight.

If you can grasp and apply this idea—I no longer am allowed to hold anyone else up to my standards—like a scrim or a template in your mind's eye, the odds of keeping a long-term relationship and being content with each other go way up. Let's face it, we can kill love easily if we expect our partners to be all things to us and keep suffocating them. We can wreck our happiness by micromanaging, attempting to change them or improve them or manipulate and mold them. Leave your magnificent man alone or your wonderful wife alone. Each of you is perfect in Spirit's eyes (some say He brings us together so we can grind against each other and in turn polish each other to our maximum brilliance).

I write to my Higher Power and I ask to be shown reality, and pray to be guided to take unselfish and loving actions only. Once I have clarity on my part, I ask my sweetheart to try this process, but only once, please. Don't beg for love or try to force a solution. Remember, a request is not a demand.

Looking at myself and evaluating my words, deeds, and wants helps me to take responsibility for my life, and helps me see how I put myself in a position to be hurt. If nothing more comes to my awareness, at least I know that I am not a victim anymore.

Usually, the women I've coached see right away how they did not take care of themselves because of their fears of losing the guy or pushing them away. Whoever does this self-reflection is the partner that sets the tone of all communication. No matter what happens for the couple, their love and affections toward each other are never wasted. Compromise is inevitable in a solid relationship. I do not believe in one partner controlling the other. The only healthy surrendering of self is made to the God of your own understanding. If you are stuck with a partner who insists on domination, leave them. Experience has proven to me that if I experience troubles and tension for the majority of the time while in a relationship, it is not the right path or the right person, and I must change my course.

If I do stay, I must decide to not take offense at someone else's words or lack of words. Their actions or lack of actions is another tip-off that my decision may have been impulsive and unrealistic. I must always look at myself first to see if I need to take an action or change my attitude.

I have coached at least twenty women, young and old, and maybe three or four men through their love crises and helped them to take charge of their emotional and financial love relations. Utilize, don't analyze or romanticize or fantasize. Use the tools of writing and the ideas and exercises in this book. Reclaim your God-given powers, and the right love partner will find you. Don't cheat yourself out of the love you deserve. The worst place to be is on the fence. Should I stay? Should I go? Follow your gut. Make a decision and do the next right thing.

Genevieve was a successful civil attorney. She bore a remarkable resemblance to Princess Di and wore clothes to try to look like her. She was actively dating to find the perfect husband. Her definition of perfect was kept hidden from most everyone, save me. She approached dating the way she approached her legal cases. Genevieve did her research and placed herself in locations where her type of ideal man would be found. You probably guessed her criteria was a high income. Gentlemen with lots of money and no baggage. That was the ticket. Their age, their health – none of it really mattered to her. Even the amount of time the fellow had to give to her wouldn't be an issue, or so she confided in me.

No surprise, after four or five months, she found her man. Milton was his name. Also, a successful lawyer. An older man, he was elated by the beautiful Genevieve and showered her with gifts and trips. He was self-conscious, though, of his wrinkles and their age difference, and had a facelift to feel better about himself. After six months, Genevieve began growing apart from him. She came out of her denial and saw herself for the first time. She didn't like what she saw. Milton had all her requirements, but Genevieve now wanted something more. She wanted real love based on her intrinsic worth, not just her looks.

She ended her affair with Milton. She took some time off dating and did a lot of coaching with me. While working on a case, she met her client's brother, and a true spark began. Genevieve's new criteria was now to meet a man of substance and confidence, close to her age, and interested in creating a family. Jamie was handsome and funny and physically fit. Two years later, they wed, and now they have two adorable daughters, eighteen months and three years, and are living their dream in Colorado. Genevieve and Jamie are wildly happy and communicate beautifully with each other.

Another time, Tom came to me. He came to me through a mutual friend. He was unhappy with his girlfriend and just kept thinking she'd be perfect if she'd just take his loving advice. He loved her, and he just wanted them to be on the same page, he kept telling me. They had different life schedules. She was a late bird, and he was an early riser. He just couldn't, or wouldn't, accept that that was how her internal clock worked. After we coached, and he internalized the concept that he could only control himself and his standards, he was able to let Maggie live up to her own standards and by her own schedule. Tom even realized that having a couple of hours to himself in the morning helped him to take care of himself. The time they spent together after that was met with gratitude and fun, and they had a great relationship.

25. I Am the Gem, the Jewel, the Prize, the Party

IT MAY SEEM ridiculous, but after twenty-three years of affirming I am the gem, the jewel, the prize, the party, I actually believe it. I now own all those attributes.

Growing up as I did, with parents who rarely praised me, I did all sorts of reckless things, often dangerous activities in my teens and twenties, and through my thirties, trying to feel that I was valuable and worthy, and that I had earned my "place" in life. My father, the epitome of low self-esteem, had modeled his obsessive-compulsive love for my mother, and she was a narcissist. I always sought approval from men, boys really, boys like my father who were not altogether sure of their worth and their ability to be successful at their careers.

In the last seventeen years, I've helped at least twenty or more women and several men build their self-confidence and their self-esteem. Yes, helped them to discover their full potential in business and in their romantic relationships. I encourage my men readers out there to write your own affirmation, from the male point of view, much like "the gem, the jewel, the prize, the party," and try something like, "I am the hero, the champion, the ultimate provider, the king and guardian of my life." By using an affirmation to reprogram the unflattering and unkind ideas that my ego throws at me on a daily moment-to-moment basis—the more I can assert my powerful, positive statements—the less I will be seduced into beating myself up so much that I need to pursue destructive behaviors, i.e., drinking, drugging, sexing, buying, eating, and escaping my negative mind.

No, once I love and approve of myself, which is a never-ending practice, I'm more free and more likely to attract a mate with an equal amount of self-love and self-esteem. Water seeking its own level is in fact, true. My life is what my thinking and my actions make of it.

Our basic needs as humans are to be seen, heard, and somewhat understood and appreciated by our society and our intimate relationships. When I find my self-love, and I find a power greater than I am to rely on, I give myself the foundation for a pleasant, fulfilling life journey. Life has very little to do with money and possessions. A great life has everything to do with our attitudes and what we tell ourselves throughout every given day.

I periodically ask myself what is motivating my behaviors, and ask myself if I'm satisfied by the consequences and outcomes of that behavior. My habit of stepping outside of my head and looking at my life as if it were a movie is a very rewarding endeavor. Most people live their lives in a bumper car capacity, bumping into this and going there, and bumping into that person and being this. So by periodically asking myself these questions, and checking in with myself and with my Higher Power, I'm cultivating what keeps me from going numb and going into a trance—like when you're driving alone in your car and you don't know how you got to where you are, or what road you took, and you aren't even aware of how long it took, plus you were oblivious to what was going on outside your window.

Designing my life is far better. It's a far better pathway than the random, ricocheting manner that puts us in a passive mode or at the mercy of others' existences and their unexamined, impulsive lives. Living from my Source, living from my core beliefs and personal values puts the reins back in my hands. The road can be bumpy or tricky or end suddenly, but I still know how I want to steer. I'm at choice, instead of chaos.

SECTION 3

Life How–Tos

I.   *Dating and Love*

Are You Ready?

TRUE LOVE IS a connection that is at once creative, emotional, spiritual, and exhilarating. However, true love's hypnotic state does quiet down eventually. I can teach you how to keep the fire forever burning and your passions in your love life together as a couple fun and fulfilling all the days of your life. Does that sound impossible? Does that sound like a tall order? In my experience it's not impossible. It's attainable...absolutely attainable. You deserve to find your True Love!

Are you ready to find the love of your life, or to rephrase, have you sat quietly and listened deeply with your heart and felt your true love pulling you closer? Or do you toss and turn in bed and wake up and find yourself with your arm outstretched reaching for the one! Instead of knowing loneliness, it is time to get out there and get into action and you know it!!! All the waiting is over. Cast off your doubt and tell your inner critic and your nagging naysayer to take an extended vacation.

You and I have a mission to find the love of your life!

Some of us have known real love, but now it's gone either by death or some other circumstance. Yet we remember, and no matter how busy we keep ourselves or how many accomplishments or material acquisitions we accumulate, we can't pretend anymore that that is enough. We must give way to this deep yearning and find our true love, our soul mate. Finding true love is not a child's fairytale; it is our destiny, and I will take you by the hand and make sure you find your life partner. I have created a simple seven-step system to help you find the love of your life.

Picture a cool night gazing deeply into a roaring fire, just sitting silently enjoying the moment with your partner at your side. How about late-night snack time hot chocolate and popcorn...just you and your sweetheart. Envision sunrises standing in Hawaii gazing out over the crater, just the two of you... Can you feel the cool morning air as you see the sunrise? This is what life is all about!

Beautiful moments, beautiful memories, beautiful magic, and beautiful movement towards each other and a life that has meaning. For those of you who have not yet come to know true love, my system will take all the confusion and fear out of the process. Get ready for the adventure you have been waiting for! Love makes everything better! With love in your life, it is as if every moment turns from black-and-white into Technicolor!

You can be a superstar or the wealthiest woman on the earth or have more golf trophies than any other person alive, but if you lack love it feels empty and incomplete. Sure, falling in love isn't everything...you can help the poor and the suffering. But just imagine how glorious it would feel to do this kind of work with your true love. Yes, shoulder-to-shoulder working to help Mother Earth.

Here is a list of questions to help you identify all the things that you've used to keep yourself away from trying to meet people and trying to find your true love:

- ❦ Do you worry that there's no one out there for you?

- ❦ Do you fear that you missed the boat and that there's nobody left? That all the good ones are gone now or already taken?

- ❦ Do you resist the notion that you are the perfect age to find your true-life partner?

- ❦ Do you feel that your looks won't attract your ideal mate?

- ❦ Do you secretly feel your lack of higher education will make you seem less interesting?

- ❦ Do you suspect that your poor dating or relationships in the past have left you jaded and that you can't be fun anymore?

- ❦ Do you obsess about your imperfections and fear that your dates will see and reject you because of all your so-called flaws?

- ❦ Do you become timid and afraid to converse because you have nothing to say?

- ❦ Do you think that you have to be young in order to be sexy to other people?

- ❦ Do you fear that true love is for the young and naïve people?

- ❦ Do you not have any time for love, or is your schedule too overloaded?

- ❦ Do you think you'll never find anyone to replace the one you lost?

- ❦ Do you dread the whole dating experience and dressing up to go out and going on multiple dates?

If you answered yes to any of these, you are my ideal client. I want to help you…let me!

How to Use Love Skills: Why We Need Them

MY OBSERVATION OVER the years from talking to tons of people and interviewing hundreds of singles and married people and love partners is most people are clueless about what they want and need in a true partnership. That's the reason we need to have skills.

I decided to put forth this list of common male and female love and hate behaviors. It's difficult to get along and stay in love with our mates, because none of us really got a guidebook. So my lists are my attempt to be the guide and hopefully enlighten partners about what each other wants when it comes to their love affair.

So many of us resent and resist what our mates seem to need, because we don't have any idea why our mates want them or really need them. So the way to break through our ignorance and our spiritual arrogance and our insatiable need to change or control each other must first be clarified and understood. My lists are far from all-inclusive, but I hope they will illuminate a good amount of the gender roles' needs and what we are doing, and what the right way is, and how we can improve. Please feel free to elaborate and create your own personal lists. I'd love for you to go to my website, www.coachdeborahdowney.com and share them on my fan page. I'm always willing and happy to have input!

How to Determine Love vs. Obsession

I SOUGHT LOVE, I thought, not seeing that what I really needed was a sense of self-worth and a large dose of validation. Consequently, I was entrenched in a pernicious trap of looking for love from men that lacked self-worth themselves and were in no way capable of infusing any overflow of love, because they were continually seeking their own need for achieving greatness emotionally, socially, and most importantly, financially. This frivolous endeavor is not gender-specific by any means. Women can be equally self-absorbed and self-seeking, as many kind, generous, loving, albeit obsessively driven, men will attest.

The desperate need to be loved by someone who has no desire or intention or even willingness to try to love you back is the definition of obsession, and has no resemblance whatsoever to love. Love is an action, an energy, a gift, an expression of oneness and self-sacrifice, and an expansion of continuous gratitude and praise. Obsession leads to feelings of worthlessness and feels restrictive. Love has no container and continues to multiply.

Tortured and crazy, outrageous, undisciplined sex does not define love, especially to narcissistic men or women who become determined to gather and control the hearts and luscious bodies of as many devotees as possible. These people have a fear of enmeshment and feelings of constriction, and abhorrence for being controlled and having demands placed upon them.

When a needy woman or man, with little or no self-worth or self-esteem, becomes seduced into surrendering their body to such a tormentor, this needy folk's fear of abandonment hits the objectified person's fear of enmeshment straight on. The dance of death is in full swing, and nobody gets to be happy, ever. The basic values of women wanting community and commitment clashes immediately with the man's need for freedom and a desire to keep exploring and gathering more and all of life's adventures. Timing also plays a huge part when looking for someone to share your life with. Many of us like to nest and experience the joys of motherhood, and they don't want to traverse the globe. Many men thrill for challenges to overcome and seek new horizons to encounter.

Our love desires and expectations keep changing during life, and it can be extremely difficult to navigate our love relationships along with the twists and turns life spikes us with right between the eyes. Most of us are clueless about the various transitions ahead of us in our twenties, for sure, but also all the coming decades as well. No one ever talked to me about considering money and careers and parenting and health and finances and debt and other people's family traditions and lifelong goals, or their aspirations or my aspirations when seeking a lover, boyfriend, or husband.

Yet, all of those factors above can make or break all relationships, and it only takes one, but usually becomes many trouble sources from above. I highly suggest checking out your motives, and from time to time listening deeply when starting a new relationship. Men really do tell you what they want pretty quickly. If they say they don't really want a girlfriend, a wife, a career, a family, they mean it. Don't try to force a round peg into a square opening.

If they are particularly charming, and the sex is mind-blowing, it won't have any effect on helping him to reconsider. Once you become addicted to him, it will take one year for every three months you stay stuck to him to get over him when he tosses you aside like a used tissue.

Personally, once I got free of my tormentor at age thirty-two, I have never been remotely interested in this kind of man since. I call them "Peter Pan." They never want to grow up, and they don't.

I understand that men face Lolita-type women in a similar fashion. These femme fatales can wrap a man's soul around her pinkie finger with a bat of her fake eyelashes. No love required for these gals who want only money, power, and fame. Women who are so intoxicating, men are virtually paralyzed. These women— usually beautiful, but not always—will take your blood and inhale your soul. Here, I ask you to be honest with yourself, fellows. Do you really think she could find you provocative and desirable? If the answer isn't yes, then do yourself a favor and find a girl who you could wake up to and trust and laugh with. You deserve to be loved for yourself, not what you can buy for her or do for your lover's career. Women are not expensive pets or livestock to be bought and sold, either. You cheat yourself when you barter or beg or steal for love.

How to Rethink Dating

DATING IS FUN, especially nowadays with the Internet. Internet dating is an amazing way to pre-qualify potential mates in a much quicker, less costly, and far less cumbersome way. What I really loved was being able to state, right out in front, what I was seeking, if it was a monogamous mate for keeps, or someone to just hang out with now and then, or did I want somebody to accompany me to events as a companion?

Well, there are, of course, pitfalls to online dating. People do lie, or use photos of themselves from years prior. Some scoundrels are even married. Writing the profile, my profile, and describing what I'm seeking can be somewhat of a chore, and frustrating as well. I like to ask my friends how they see me, and craft my own bio using their descriptions of how they perceive me.

I had all the typical negative thinking initially, but reminded myself that I was open to love again, now that I had fully grieved my husband's passing twenty-eight months before. But my ego wanted to convince me that nobody would want to go out with me because I'm old, number one, and number two, because I have MS.

Well, this is where my well-practiced positive affirmation, "I am the gem, the jewel, the prize, the party," really helped me a great deal, because I believe it. My mindset was open, and not needy or desperate for love, and I knew deep in my soul that spending time in my company would be a blessing to anyone I chose to be with and date. That said, my first year of dating was kind of average. Nothing really toe-curling. My experience changed a lot, though, when I posted my last profile and chose very specific physical, financial parameters for my potential mate, and specified that they had to be a non-smoker and a non-drinker. And that's what I was determined to find.

Once I got my target clarified, fate just provided the rest. My true love appeared, and he took my breath away. He has told me that he felt dizzy when we first locked eyes on our first date. It was really pretty easy to get men to contact me, but a few times, they actually said, "No, thanks," when they were contacted by email, and several didn't respond at all once I told them that I had multiple sclerosis.

The temptation, of course, is to obsess and keep checking on a daily basis who's responding, and that is something that I do not recommend. But my ego was constantly trying to undermine my dating pursuits. I had to remind myself often that I only need one man—my Mr. Right. I don't need twenty. It's a numbers game. So I persevered with an attitude of openness and trust. I run my mind, and I think in a positive way. My mind doesn't run me. I kept fear and worry out of my mindset.

How to Internet Date

WRITE AN INTERESTING bio. Tell a story about a small victory you might have had as a child, or write about your big dreams, or write about your wish list, or your bucket list.

Don't go into wine tasting, like it is a hobby or a sport.

Make sure your photo is current. No more than a year or two old.

Try and write so it sounds like you. Don't try to be cool or clever; just be real.

Check your spelling and ask your friends to describe what they like about you, and use that as a description.

When you do speak to people on the phone, never ask them for money. Remember to take dating slow. If someone says they love you, and you have not even been on a date with them, they're most likely just trying to scam you, and they're probably in another country with a phony picture and a made-up story to scam you.

When you do decide to meet someone, pick a public place in the daytime. Take your own car. Ladies, never pick up a date. If they don't have a car, forget it.

I talked with this one fellow who was obsessed with wanting to cut my long, blonde hair. He offered to cut my hair, and my friends' hair, too. I did not meet this man. Just too weird, thank you.

I met and married a fabulous husband by using plentyoffish.net, a free online dating service in the Marin area. Over the course of my eighteen months, I had more dates than I ever had growing up. And the fact that I could see photos and bios more than once a day was great. I tried eHarmony and match.com, and met nice men, all pretty nice guys, but none of them set my heart on fire. I was a widow of two years and probably would not have begun dating were it not that a man I met in a religious setting had his eyes obsessed on me, and he pursued me. He was a big, gentle bear of a man, and I had no attraction whatever to him, but I did enjoy the attention of a man, and his efforts to win me over were greatly appreciated because I missed the attention. His attentions reminded me of how great it is to find and to be loved, to feel loved and wanted.

When I met my current husband, Ray, I had been widowed since March of 2007.

What Worked, and What to Avoid

Well, some of the things that I did that really helped are as follows:

- ❮ Great pictures showing my face and my body.

- ❮ Writing an interesting bio.

- ❮ Describing exactly what I wanted in my partner.

- ❮ Listing my personal hobbies and likes and dislikes.

- ❮ Adding in a story from my life that revealed my preferences, my talents, or my sense of funny humor.

- ❮ You can also share what inspires you, or a goal that shows your passion or foreign activity, or a charity that you're highly motivated by, or higher learning, or a project you're excited about.

- ❮ Looks really matter, so I don't hide or misrepresent how I look. I wore clothes that are the same kinds of clothes that I wear when I go on a date, or you'd see me in going to the market.

What doesn't work, assuming of course that you want to find a lasting relationship:

- ❮ Pictures that are dark, or are far away and don't show your face.

- ❮ No pictures of your body.

- ❮ Clothes that are too revealing, or nudity should be avoided.

- ❮ Pictures of you drinking or stoned in a bar or at home, half-dressed.

- ❮ Writing about sex.

- ❮ Talking about wine, beer, or wanting to be helped financially.

- ❮ Living with your parents.

- ❮ Lying about anything.

- Trying to sound "cool."
- Writing about religion or politics.
- Avoid bad spelling. Boy, that makes you appear stupid.
- Sounding arrogant.
- Sounding needy.
- Sounding like a big shot.

All of these things should be avoided. They are red flags.

What Men Love

- Men love to come home to their beautiful, well-put-together lover, looking like she did when they were dating.
- Men love to be appreciated and admired.
- Men love to be complimented.
- Men like to be looked at when asked something important.
- Men love when you suggest an outing to something that you know that they love, like a sports event or fishing or whatever it is that they love, and you suggest it.
- Men like it when you discuss concerns before 9:00PM, and they even appreciate it more when you set up the time by asking ahead if you can have a talk together.
- Men love to be touched, kissed, and hugged.
- Men love when you initiate the sex.
- Men love to be told, "I want you."
- Men love long backrubs, head-stroking, foot massages.
- Men love treats—sexual, of course, and also objects and thoughtful cards and yummy treats to eat.

What Men Hate

◖ Men seem to hate their girlfriend looking sloppy and dumpy.

◖ Men hate to be jumped on the moment they get home and walk in the front door.

◖ Men hate to be late and wait for you to be ready.

◖ Men hate to be asked the same question over and over and over.

◖ Men hate being managed.

◖ Men hate being mothered, if they're healthy, that is.

◖ Men hate being interrupted.

◖ Men hate being ignored.

◖ Men hate being quizzed or hounded.

◖ Men hate holidays when they are expected to buy gifts, and it's an obligation, like Christmas or Valentine's Day could be, but if you follow a certain step or two, it can be good. The best way I've found is to discuss the budget and agree on an amount you will both spend. Or you could even decide not to do gifts at all!

◖ Men hate being lied to or manipulated.

◖ Men also hate to feel that they're in a game or a competition.

◖ And men really seem to hate it when I insist, or we insist, on wearing something that they've already told us that they don't like to see us in.

What Women Love

◖ Women love to hear that they are important, appreciated, and that they are beautiful and desired by their man.

◖ Women love it when you give generously and joyfully.

❨   Women love to be acknowledged for their cooking, cleaning, and decorating of their home.

❨   Just as men enjoy spontaneous quick sex, women are deeply moved by little, girly gifts, candy, flowers.

❨   Women love to be told that they feel so good to hold, or smell so delicious.

❨   Women love it when their men verbalize their approval and their man is concerned and says things in a kind manner.

❨   Women love to know where they stand.

❨   Women love to be able to, and encouraged to, express and feel their feelings.

❨   Women love when their partner also feels and can express his feelings.

❨   Women love to be touched gently, and women love to submit to the man that they love and trust.

❨   Women love to be held.

❨   Women love to hear, "We're in this together."

❨   Women love to feel capable and encouraged when they take up a new path or a new idea or old idea, or new skill or belief.

❨   Women like to feel that they are the most important person in their man's world.

❨   Women love when their fella seduces them just as much as when they are the seducer.

❨   Women love to be creative and validated by their man. Creative can be in various areas—cooking, being an artist, a builder, a designer, a gardener, a mother, performing crafts, like knitting, sewing, jewelry-making, being a fashionista, being a writer, a singer, a dancer, and a creative wife are just a few.

❮ Women love words of expression and details. They love it when you tell them things, especially when it comes in a loving tone.

❮ Women like to give, so long as they are treated fairly and their time and efforts are respected, and you also express your gratitude.

❮ Women love to feel protected and safe.

❮ Women love to have their man make plans for a special romantic getaway.

❮ Women love to be invited to participate when their man makes plans.

❮ Women love any action that's taken when at least she's included in the discussion.

❮ Women love to have a community of women friends.

❮ Women love to be heard and feel seen by their lover.

❮ Women love "we" time and "me" time and random dream time.

What Women Hate

❮ Women hate when her man talks to other people and they don't get acknowledged or introduced to them.

❮ Women hate to be bullied or hit or left, and treated like a used tissue.

❮ Women hate vulgarity and cruelty of any kind towards anything and everything living.

❮ Women hate angry outbursts or rageful stomping off, or any other rageful behavior like throwing your fist into the wall and frightening them.

❮ Women hate vagueness when it comes to where they are in their relationship, or worse, they hate liars or cheaters or exploiters or being manipulated by a man they love.

❮ Women hate being criticized and given endless orders, or constantly being teased, or worse, made to feel a fool when her man is hanging out with his buddies, or when he mocks her to her peers or her parents or her family.

❮   Women hate when men ignore them and won't talk to them. And by the way, women remember every mean remark and comment forever.

❮   Women hate to be compared to their man's former lovers, and women hate to be compared to his mother.

❮   Women hate when her man forgets her birthday or their anniversary.

❮   Women hate when her man makes fun of her TV shows.

❮   Women hate when her man ridicules her church or spiritual practice.

❮   Women hate it when her man sends letters to old girlfriends and Christmas cards or emails or phones them on a regular basis.

❮   Women hate it when her man looks at sex magazines and porno and watches porn on the Internet.

❮   Women hate it when her man is obsessed with sports or his hobbies or his work or his children from a previous marriage.

❮   Women hate when men are inconsiderate. Period.

How I Met, Married, and Manifested the Man I'd Always Dreamed Of

I STARTED DATING by using the three main dating services and met five or six men and went on three dates, usually, with most of them, but I really had no real connection to any of them— no chemical attraction, no deep feelings for any of them beyond friendship. I was on the verge of quitting my search, when I saw Ray's picture and sent him a hello message. There he was, this tall, long-legged man, stretched out on top of his brand-new Harley. A magnificent Harley. And then another picture I saw was him sitting on his mustard leather, L-shaped couch. He was living in Napa at the time.

My ten months of practice dating and all my previous searches had taught me how to just post messages and then forget about it. I will confess that I was a bit obsessed initially, constantly running home to see who had responded to me. Finally, I understood that if I was destined to meet my true love, it could take a little longer.

Well, I'm happy to report my search after that only took two days. Ray and I emailed back and forth a few weeks, and it was immediately apparent we had an amazing chemistry. The sound of each other's voice was seductive and made us want more and more interaction. We had our first date in my city of Novato, California, on Grant Street, our town's main street. We decided to meet for an early dinner at the charming, tiny Italian restaurant, and I got a parking spot directly in front of the bistro. As I emerged from my hybrid Highlander, I saw this tall man coming out of the front door of the restaurant to meet me. I was excited and bashful as I watched him approaching me.

He had a full beard and a mustache. He was so handsome, movie star handsome, in fact, and I was swooning inside. This had never happened for me before! I felt scared and delighted at the same time.

My mother passed away four hours later that same evening, February 1st, 2010. The timing of these two major events in my life was exquisite. My mother has and will always be the biggest influence in my life. Yes, as my mother walked on, dear Ray walked in.

Ray and I had such a lovely, yet brief, courtship. We would stand just inside my front door hugging and kissing for forty-five minutes whenever we ended a date. We waited a good six weeks before jumping into bed. Our physical connection was electric, and after about four weeks, he said, "When are we going to get naked?" I burst into laughter, as it did not sound pushy or lecherous, just funny to me. I told him I wanted to wait at least until after my mother's memorial was passed. Somehow, it just didn't seem right not to wait.

I had had a "keep your distance" attitude with all of my prior suitors, but one day a switch flipped inside me, and I really had a major shift in feelings towards Ray after that night.

A few days later, Ray picked The Little River Inn, for our first "overnight," as he called it. I looked it up online, and immediately became excited for the weekend he had planned. The Inn was a perfect size, and incredibly romantic. The ocean views—spectacular. We felt like two giddy teenagers, sneaking away for the weekend, as we drove up the coast to get there.

As we drove up the coast to get there, the awkwardness was palpable, yet our desire was stronger. Instead of holding back, I wanted to jump his bones! I was no longer afraid to love again. I was confident to move forward with Ray. We'd had a fantastic gourmet dinner at the hotel that night, and it was close to bedtime. The idea came to me to suggest a round or two of strip poker. And guess what? I won. Ray wound up in his skivvies and socks. We laughed. We had an amazing night. That's all I'm going to say about that.

Roughly nineteen days after that, I broke my right femur bone. Yes, I broke my femur jumping out of bed and running to the bathroom. I slipped and fell. Another inch higher, and I would've had to have a total hip replacement. It was the first broken bone I'd ever had in my entire life. Ray was again unbelievably kind and helpful. He even reconfigured my shower so it would have easy access for when I came back from rehab. I stayed in skilled nursing, doing rehab for six weeks. He visited me and brought me yummy treats, as I was losing weight.

During this stay in the skilled nursing, I had a daily flow of friends visiting and taking care of my pets, Jessie James, Toby, and

Bodhi. This fall that I'd had and the broken femur made me question, number one, if I'd ever walk again, and number two, whether Ray would leave me and move on in his life. We talked about this, and he admitted the thought had crossed his mind, but he said, "I love you. And I'm here." By May, I was walking and driving again.

Ray sold his home in Napa and moved into my condo in Novato July 1st, and we began searching for a house to buy and live in together. We moved into our current home in Camino, California, also known as Apple Hill, just north of Placerville. Our marriage took place May 6, 2012, in our front yard.

Between us, we have six grown children, both of us parenting two boys and one daughter. They all are just about the same ages, too. I had written a "man wanted" ad. It was a list. I had written it one and a half years before we found each other, and he fit my criteria perfectly. I have included it so others may try it. It was easy for me to articulate what I wanted because I was crystal clear on what I did not want.

I discovered that mature people over fifty are rid of many of the hang-ups that younger people face, and I saw from my dating experience, folks seemed to really crave love, affection, touching, and companionship. The profiles and the bios of the men I found on these sites were so similar, yet were written as if the man thought he was unique in this way. People really want to be loved and return love. Most of us know we can kill love. Love is never wasted, though, or needs to be regretted for not succeeding. The relationships I have had have all taught me so much about myself. I am grateful for all my past experiences.

The clearer I understand what love is, and the more I learn to love myself, the better my choices and selections have gotten. Once I realized that I am responsible for my reactions and my ultimate attitudes and happiness, I knew it wasn't my job to save, fix, or make you happy, either. We each are responsible for ourselves. Period.

My Definition of Dating

DATING IS AN opportunity to meet and be open to learning more about a person.

It is helpful to know what you are hoping to do and get from the relationship and to be truthful to yourself and also to the person you will meet.

It is better to choose a date that seeks the same goals.

My list of dos and don'ts for dating:

- ❨ Do approach dating with a sense of adventure and discovery
- ❨ Do wear clothes that you feel attractive in, but they must be comfortable
- ❨ Do dress nicely and not sleazy
- ❨ Do make an effort and to be present and open-minded
- ❨ Do be over any previous relationships and be available to find someone new/different
- ❨ Do be polite and considerate and truly curious about your date
- ❨ Do tell two or more people who is taking you out and where you are going
- ❨ Do be yourself and ask them all about what they are searching for
- ❨ Do meet in the day, if possible, for tea and a light snack
- ❨ Do look like your picture
- ❨ Do know where you are going and when you need to be back before you leave on date
- ❨ Do date two or three woman/men while looking and no commitment has been made
- ❨ Do ask questions and share the conversation
- ❨ Do bring your own car
- ❨ Do bring some money

❨ Do listen closely...people tell you what they believe

❨ Do keep the date short—no more taking hostages

❨ Do ask about your date's family, i.e., any children, how many, exes, employment, parents

❨ Do ask about your date's health, spiritual beliefs, or connections to groups and interests

❨ Do let your date know if you are interested in meeting with them again

---

❨ Don't be rude, late, selfish, act superior, lie, steal, or behave cool and aloof

❨ Don't dominate the conversation or expect them to propel conversation

❨ Don't audition for love

❨ Don't show off

❨ Don't pressure or demand or compare your date to other singles while on date

❨ Don't go to the bathroom for thirty minutes or see a friend and abandon your date

❨ Don't rush the date or drag it out

❨ Don't over-order expensive food unless you are paying for it

❨ Don't drink too much or at all if you don't

❨ Don't feel obliged to hug, kiss, or go somewhere else with them

❨ Don't forget to say "thank you" and "nice meeting you"

❨ Don't criticize, control, or complain

❨ Don't ignore your date or text or talk on the phone

Man or Woman Want Ad
List of Wants for My Dream Man *(my list—write your own)*

THIS IS MY want ad to the universe to bring me the man of my dreams.

Wanted:

☆ *A man that is kind to me and my family, and peaceful in nature.*

☆ *A man that is sexy to me and turned on by me.*

☆ *A man that is loyal to me in every way, and takes my side above all others.*

☆ *A man that makes a really good living and keeps on top of his financial picture.*

☆ *A man that is humble and teachable, patient with me and my family and his family and the world.*

☆ *A man that works at a moderate pace and does his work well, but not as a perfectionist and compulsively or obsessively.*

☆ *A man that knows who he is and takes responsibility for his actions and attitudes.*

☆ *A man that is supportive to his fellow man and me and my family and his family, but always puts himself and me and my family first.*

☆ *A man that is in touch with his feelings and acknowledges mine.*

☆ *A man that is authentic and honest with himself and forth-right and open with me.*

☆ *A man that is generous, playful, warm, and sexy, and really available to me as his partner.*

☆ *A man that is even-tempered and balanced and likes himself, and takes good care of himself, and just adores me.*

☆ *A handsome, fit man, with wonderful hair, who smells great.*

☆ *A man that is free of sexual hang-ups.*

☆ *A man that is well-read, that loves music, that loves theatre.*

☆ *A man that has a great job he loves and is proud of what he's doing, and if he's artistic, oh my god, that's even better.*

☆ *A man that likes to travel.*

☆ *A man that likes to entertain friends with parties, like I do.*

☆ *A man that likes to take me out and pays with no weirdness about it, like the good old days.*

☆ *A man that enjoys my company and my femininity.*

☆ *A man that always maintains his health, his diet, his weight, and hygiene and dental care, and otherwise says what he means, means what he says, and he doesn't say mean things.*

☆ *A man that is spiritually fit, meditates, reads, prays, and has no opinion about what my practices are when it comes to faith, and doesn't quiz me or try to change me.*

☆ *A man that has an up, bright, optimistic outlook.*

☆ *A man that doesn't reminisce about his ex-wives or other lovers, yet will readily answer questions if I ask.*

☆ *A man that takes his own inventory, which means he reflects on his words and his actions to see whether or not he's happy with how he's being, and he doesn't take my inventory; he lets me do that.*

☆ *I want a man that, when he's wrong, promptly admits it
   and makes amends, and it's not just words. He changes.*

☆ *A man that is someone I can look up to, physically and mentally, and he's my hero.*

☆ *A man that's someone who loves me. He loves to hold me
   and touch me, and I love to hold him.*

How to Unleash Your Inner Vixen/Viking and Create Your Ultimate Passion with Your Partner, Mate, and Spouse

DURING THE PAST twenty-three years, I have coached lots of men and women to achieve true joy and success in their love relation-ships, including sizzling, hot sex together. I've come up with four steps I use to assist eager couples to create rockin' sex lives. We will go into each step individually, but here they are collectively: Per-mission, Play, Place, and the fourth step includes Pleasure, Passion, and Performance.

Okay. Sex starts in our minds and leads us to the physical actions that bring us to ecstasy. Sex is an exchange of energy and a release and a surrender. The French call orgasm "a little death," in fact. Men and women are hardwired to engage in this dance of domination and surrender. The pursuer and the captive.

The first and most important aspect in sex is permission. I need to give myself permission first, before I can invite and/or flirt or seduce my partner. Permission will only be granted if I am clear of resentment and I feel safe and I am free of expectation. Asking myself what I want from the relationship, what is its purpose, will often open the gates of willingness and supersede all the excuses that my low self-esteem and/or apathy can throw up at me: I'm too fat, too old, I'm not sexy, I'm not perfect…but when you remember your purpose is love and a deep desire to share intimacy, you can tell your ego to shut up. I tell myself I'm sexy, desirable, and I'm ready. I decide I want to enjoy my body and my lover's body.

Our imperfections make us adorable and unique. Throw out all the old experiences and give yourself permission to abandon all control and perfectionism. When you give yourself permission in this way, you will feel the urge to merge, I guarantee it.

All right, so now we're at step two, and this is play. And play sets the tone. When we play with our partners, we have flipped the green light on switch, and our lover can sense it, even if we don't say anything. I want to add that I know how fast-paced life is today. Schedules to keep, obligations to meet daily. However, the need for play is so important for our sensuality, I choose to think of play like I do brushing my teeth on a daily basis. Flirting and complimenting my lover throughout the day, telling him or her you love their butt, legs, eyes, lips. When I tell my lover, "I want you now," it's a huge turn-on. Even if they need to leave, letting them know that you'll be waiting will send them out the door with Eros's spark in their mind and loins.

Touch your partner in sensual ways throughout the day, all week long. Stand and hug and scratch each other's back and look into each other's eyes. Buy special, provocative lingerie, and fellas, buy some sexy underwear for us, too. Walk around naked in front of your lover, posing and teasing, telling them exactly what you want to do to them. The more you emphasize the things they do that you like and how amazing they make your body feel, the better you try to phrase things from the positive, the better it gets. Telling them your fantasy of how you see them doing something you really want and asking, "Can we try that, baby?" is so much better than, "Do this, do that, no, not there," guiding and directing. You share something about how your body feels so yummy after your shower, or after they shower, or, "Do you want to take a shower together, sugar?" Tell your partner how hot they look and taste when they are sweaty and grimy, and that that is a total turn-on. Be grateful, ladies, when your lover grabs your boobs, your ass, your crotch. Grab his crotch or butt back, too.

I played strip poker with Ray on our first sleepover, as he calls it, and it was so erotic. Oh my god. Let each other know one or two times a day that you love their body. Stroke them. Hug them. All right. You get the idea. And women really respond to words, gentlemen. Tell your lover that you like the way she looks, that she's beautiful, and she'll just be so ready for you. For men, men love to be visually stimulated, so show them, ladies. Give them what you got.

The third step is place. Change things up. Use different rooms in your house. Set the stage with candles, scents. Plan out times for long, undisturbed foreplay and pampering, but then be ready for sex at all times so that you can have a quickie, and girls, you can initiate the quickie. That's hot, hot, hot.

Adventurous sex outside, in places other than your home. Try your car. Try a place of risk, where you might get caught. Try a scandalous place. Who cares what people think? There is no age limit here, people, no matter how old and saggy you think you are, you are hot, especially if you stand in front of the mirror and tell yourself, "You are hot, baby."

The previous three steps lead to our love purpose, which is pleasure, passion, and performance. Pleasure: try new products. Use clothes that can be ripped off and torn or eaten. Use props and food and drink, but don't get drunk and high; that diminishes the effects, and your stamina, too. Stimulate each other with feathers. Tickle each other. If you do take up a quickie, don't stop and arrange things or brush your teeth. Just let go and dive in.

Passion: Stop thinking, stop talking, ladies, except for expressions and murmurs of enjoyment. Resist the urge to ask, "Is this okay?" or, "Do you love me?" or, "Am I the best?" All such neurotic questions deflate passion. Touch your own body and touch theirs on their back, arms. Grab their hair, scratch lightly on the middle of their back. Pinch their earlobes.

Now we come to performance. Whatever level of ecstasy you both reach, express gratitude for having each other. If you have embraced and followed all the above steps, I guarantee you, you will have had an amazing, intimate, and satisfying experience with your beloved. All women want to be sensual and surrender to a partner that is confident, considerate, strong, and protective. Leave the outside world and petty grievances away from your mind. Take a sex challenge and have sex seven days in a row, and take turns being the initiator. Be open-minded and adventurous. Express your feelings. And if you have unresolved issues, they can wait. Enjoy your bodies while they still work.

II.   *Working on Your Inner Self*

How to Take Care of Yourself

TAKING CARE OF myself is a multi-task practice. It involves looking at the past experiences and taking stock of errors made, and remembering what did feel good and why. This habit of self-reflection is so worthwhile and is fascinating. Morbid thoughts and guilt and regret are to be avoided.

Setting a timer and reviewing events of great impact for thirty minutes once a week is a good way to begin. I think of it as looking in the rearview mirror. I can't look too long, or I'll drive off the road. Taking stock is similar to a doctor in an operating room. He opens the patient up, finds the diseased piece, and removes it, without drama and attachment to the sick part or the patient.

Life is so hectic, and we are called to do so much daily, just to survive. It may seem impossible or unimportant to build this activity into your week. We spend so much energy with media devices, meals, shopping, games, socializing, instead of knowing and loving our own company. Just do it. Continue doing it. Make it your number one priority. By disciplining yourself for thirty minutes every week, you will unlock the door to your true self. That is the first step in loving and honoring yourself. Happiness is an inside job.

Clarity is an underrated experience. With clarity, we break out of our trances, and access our hearts, and define our wants and deep desires. By looking lovingly at my actions, feelings, and my thought processes, I become my own advocate and gain peace within.

I saw Dr. Phil on Letterman last week, and he said one out of every ten people in the U.S. is on some form of antidepressant. He also said many shouldn't be on it. I don't know, and I wouldn't begin to comment. I do know that I am not on any antidepressants, even though I was offered them twenty-three years ago, when I was diagnosed with multiple sclerosis. I opted to use the steps of several twelve-step programs to begin my self-discovery. My experiences with the programs is that they do the job for substances and bad behaviors by removing the urge, but too often, the members remain lost and despondent outside their recovery rooms, or simply exchange addictions for another addiction.

All addictions have the mental component that tells us we must satisfy this drive for the substance or the reckless behavior so that we'll exist. Merely gaining abstinence is not enough for joyful living. Freeing our minds from worry and regret is not only possible, I guarantee that you can get it.

The beautiful, liberating ideas I offer to you will give you the ways and means to control your thoughts. Instead of listening to K-F**K all day and night, you can tune into K-JOY. You can dial into clarity, finally escaping the random static in your life, in your head. The ranting of demented, disgusting tyrants of your past and present relations, employers, teachers, politicians, lovers, players, teammates, competitors, will no longer have power over you. Tragic events will become valuable blessings to be shared with others. What I share here is not intended to replace medication, twelve-step programs, therapy, religious practices, or teachings.

These ideas are meant to enhance and support everything you currently find helpful. These ideas are practical, simple, and easy to use. Along with the ideas, I will reveal several tips that I've used to accentuate and speed up my triumph over worry.

One of my best tips is to make a list of your ten top favorite memories of each of your parents. All of us have a deep need to be seen, or witnessed, and heard, and known. When I knew my father was dying of cancer, I did my list about him. I made my list based on my senses—touch, smell, taste, sound, and sight. I put it on a lovely piece of paper and used my computer and designed it with a font I thought he would like. I saw him in the hospital and read it to him. He perked up, and he took it all in fully. I did the list of my ten top favorite memories for my mother on her 75th birthday. She loved it, but didn't like that I put her age on that paper. I honored her wish, and I redid it, and I framed it. I also invite all of you to create your own way of honoring your parents—by a song, a poem, a painting, video, anything that stirs your imagination.

Sadly, I know many of you have had such horrific parents that there are no memories to recall other than the painful ones, or none at all, if you didn't know them at all. To those of you, I say, the true parent of all of us is our Creator. We can write the list from our own ten top favorite memories of love and joy.

How to Stand Up for Yourself

WE ARE ALL equal in God's eyes. We are all His/Her favorites and he loves each and every one of us madly. The drunk lying in the gutter is no less valuable to Divine Intelligence than the adorable little girl in pink tights, a tutu and ballet slippers. None of us is any better than or worse than anyone else. We have no right to kill or harm any of Spirit's kids. We have no right to control or dominate each other. Yet some do. That is not acceptable ever. Abuse of any kind, mental or physical, of any living creature is never acceptable.

An equally unacceptable behavior is to allow someone to continuously abuse you. So it is vital to learn how to identify abuse when it is happening and how to stand up for yourself with your abuser. I do someone a spiritual disservice when I allow abuse to continue from anyone in or out of my immediate family.

You may think, "Why, anybody knows when they are being abused…don't they?" Many of us have very high tolerance levels for abuse and can't recognize when it is occurring. Often these people are in so much denial, it is difficult to figure it out. However, they feel something is off even if they cannot name it. I coach people who have made a career out of being doormats for Tormentors! I help them see this pattern and break-out of the merry-go-round of fear and abuse and shame.

I always suggest not being foolish enough to ever confront a tormentor that has a weapon or a means to physically harm you or your loved ones. Let the authorities handle anything like that. Get the help you need right away.

Please don't be intimidated by bullies. You must get off the floor to stop being a doormat. It is better to be alone than permit someone to harm you.

If the abuse is verbal, tell the person "Stop it." Continue by saying that "It is not okay to speak to me that way." Don't scream or pursue them. Again say, "Stop it! Please don't speak to me like that…it is unacceptable." I learned this technique from a teacher who worked with children with autism. I have also used it when approached by an angry homeless person. It works because it is unexpected and a simple declaration.

How to Overcome Your Victim Mentality

LIFE CAN REALLY wear you down if you allow yourself to live at the mercy of what other people think of you or let them determine your worth/value. I auditioned for love/approval all my life, 'til a wise mentor showed me how I was giving away my power by letting and volunteering to pursue the stamp of approval from others: my parents, my teachers, my lovers, my bosses, my peers, and finally my children. I need only my approval and my Source's approval these days. I only accept compliments, thank you.

This process of self-reflection and self-acceptance is a lifelong endeavor, and the rewards are so worth the time, honesty, and effort it takes to truly know and love myself, but it's worth it. People can feel when they have power over you because you don't believe in yourself or are simply starved for love and approval, and they often will withhold love as a way to control you.

Once we understand that our happiness, self-love and self-forgiveness is an inside job, we can pursue them all. We are free. We will never be a victim again. This proves especially true and beneficial to us when we are breaking away from an intimate relationship. Women and men place different amounts of importance in relationship, and therefore men can usually let go of a marriage seemingly with greater ease. The symbolism of the bee pollinating many flowers comes to mind. The standards for monogamous agreement carries different levels of priority for that very reason.

Having said that, I have had quite a few male clients who were, in their perception, wildly disrespected and betrayed by a cheating wife or lover. We each have given love, fidelity, and commitment differing levels of importance. My experience has shown me that people really do reveal who they are quite openly and often quite

dding romance. Many of the ladies I've worked with
ᴏ me fairly early on that they saw how many red flags
their pa.....r was displaying from their interactions with them, but
chose to ignore these hints.

How I Harm Myself and How to Stop

I WAS RAISED by parents who became alcoholics over the course
of their thirties. As a result, I have been deeply affected by the
effects of alcoholism. The twelve steps of the Adult Children of
Alcoholics, as well as the Al-Anon family groups, have trans-
formed my life, and all the destructive behavior and thinking
habits that I acquired living with the active disease. I highly
recommend both programs, especially if your parents were alcoholics, but also if you were parented by dysfunctional parents of
any kind, i.e., gamblers, womanizers, workaholics, mentally or
chronically ill parents, or you were abandoned, literally, or simply
felt invisible.

I find that if you had any abuse at all, you most likely abuse
yourself personally on a daily basis. I put together a list of the
harms that I'd done myself recently for a group of adult children
I was helping, and I thought that you might benefit if you could
understand how you harm yourself by self-abandonment.

The first step to removing the damage done by internalizing
the lousy ideas and behaviors you picked up is to become aware.
Eventually, you will be able to name it, claim it, and dump it. We
don't use any of this work to confront or do any harm of any sort
to our parents. I continue to coach people through their past and
gain their freedom from themselves and to forgive themselves for
reenacting the poor choices their parents modeled for them. So
here's my list, my most recent list, of how I harm myself.

« I harm myself when I let others define my worth or my success.

« I harm myself when I put anyone else's needs in front of mine.

« I harm myself when I eat things that I know aren't healthy for me.

« I harm myself when I go into a TV coma and do not get up, and sit there all night.

« I harm myself when I go into an iPad coma and stay on the iPad all day.

« I harm myself when I get seduced by shiny objects instead of staying on my task and doing what I plan to do.

« I harm myself when I lie to you, or when I lie to me.

« I harm myself when I get angry at you.

« I harm myself when I stay up too late and I don't get my rest.

« I harm myself when I don't check in with God or any of my mentor coaches if I'm troubled about something.

« I harm myself when I label events as good or bad.

« I harm myself when I don't move enough or exercise.

« I harm myself when I think too much.

« I harm myself when I won't surrender because I enjoy suffering.

« I harm myself when I hold people up to my standards and judge them or resent them.

« I harm myself when I don't read the fine print.

« I harm myself when I compare, complain, or condemn, or try to change or control others.

« I harm myself when I rush.

« I harm myself when I procrastinate.

« I harm myself when I get distracted and fragmented.

« I harm myself when I sit too long.

(I harm myself when I stay inside and don't get outside all day.

(I harm myself when I self-justify to assuage my ego.

(I harm myself when I don't look at my calendar every morning.

(I harm myself when I spend unconsciously.

(I harm myself when I push to be perfect.

(I harm myself when I watch violence and become obsessed with bad events, or when I participate in gossip.

(I harm myself when I stay vague about my finances in my business.

How to Deal With Your Rage and Violence

THIS PIECE IS on rage and violence. People don't like to talk about rage, even though the rage topic is something we see on television and movies and read about on our IPads and in the newspaper. Rage is passed from generation to generation, and the hate of our forefathers and mothers toward differing races and cultures also can be passed from generation to generation.

The beauty of living a life of choice and design is that we don't need to accept the unacceptable anymore. The rage mechanism can be halted and aborted, much like smoking cigarettes or drinking can, with the aid of a Higher Power and our own personal willingness to do so.

I heard this man speak of his own triumph over his rage, and it changed my life forever. I was in my mid-thirties when this happened. Frankie was sort of a roughneck, and was talking about a moment of clarity he was struck with as he saw the fear in the eyes of his secretary. A moment, he said, as if time stopped, and his inner voice said, "You have no right to scream and rage at her."

I sat there, and I heard that, and from that day forward, I asked God to remove rage from me, and any of my own desires to hit or strike any living thing. My father had hit me in the face, and so I had been hitting living things up until then. So if you are a rager, or a hitter, stop it. You have no right. Get whatever help you can, but stop it.

If you can't stop it, leave the situation. End the relationship. Or turn yourself in. Don't cop out and say, "Well, that's just me. That's the way I am." No, that won't wash. Violence is sick, and it is addictive. And if you are with a rage-aholic, end it. You do someone a spiritual disservice by permitting or volunteering for abuse. What you permit, you teach. You cosign abuse if you do not leave, and become someone's punching bag. Get out. Take care of yourself. You are precious and valuable.

How to Address Worry

THERE ARE DIFFERENT forms of worry. Learning how to live without worry is a simple decision to be made daily and sometimes multiple times during a day. When we break down worry, you can see it is rarely applicable to the present. Worry pulls us into the future or rolls us back into the past.

My Higher Power lives in the now and for my Higher Power, it is always the now! Time is a manmade concept. My Higher Power is available to help me now. Worry may merely be a distraction that our egos use to keep us captive and constantly shaking in our boots. It is best to allow time to prepare well for a coming event, but let God do all the worrying and you do the work. There are many triggers that may cause us to worry. Personal worry would be something like having too exact a plan for the event we wish to take place. Expectations always lead to disappointment and tension. We can plan for the future but need to let our Divine Intelligence handle all the details and the outcome. To combat worry, we need to stay open and flexible and let go of our "plans."

Worry for our families can be stopped when we remember that each member has their own path, their own lessons, and their very own Higher Power. A surefire way to do that is to recall how much you also dislike being compared to others...or worse —controlled by or manipulated by bossy people. Instead of fussing with someone, embolden them with praise. Give them their respect and their dignity. Remember that they are unique and they have their own unique life lessons. I need not do for them what they can do for themselves. If I care more about someone's life than they do, I have crossed the line and I'm actually doing them spiritual disservice.

I set the tone and the pace of my own spiritual growth with God's help, not by the help of others. I gratefully share what I have experienced and what I've come to learn. History may give us some signposts, but each new generation has to relearn exactly the same lessons that the previous generation had to learn! Sadly, history does repeat itself.

I was a very compliant and peaceful person during my childhood. Because of that, I remained quite gullible and naïve well into my early and late twenties. I question everything these days.

I question authority and I question the rules! My questioning the rules and the whys for what happens is a new skill for me, and it has become easier for me and less stressful because I changed the way I think about the rules and the so-called status quo. I used to see questioning things as rebellious and even somewhat insulting. Now that I no longer "care" what other people think about me, I see asking questions and gaining clarity as one of the best ways to take care of myself. My worries are dispelled when I ask for details and make more informed decisions.

I hardly ever worry now because I am confident that I have the tools and the know-how to take care of myself. No matter what happens to me or my loved ones, I have a process to get rid of expectations and fear and control. Over the years, I have developed a connection to my Higher Power or my highest self, and I have come to rely on it. I really love showing others how to find their own personal connection. I am my clients' advocate and I support their process. I do not fix them! They get to do that and they have me to account to.

Worry springs up when we feel uninformed or when we know we have made a mistake and will have to pay for it. Frankly, it is always better to admit our error and ask how to make it right.

The most elementary, simplest, and wisest choice we can make when we are faced with worry is to pay the fine, do the work, or do the time. Otherwise, we sacrifice our mental attention wondering if and when the axe will fall.

Check in with your gut/intuition often and ask questions 'til you have the clarity you need either to accept a situation or figure out what you need to do to change it. Vagueness is a huge source of worry. Also, procrastination will cost you a huge amount of time and shame and often money. too.

It's best to learn to stay where your feet are planted in the present. Worrying about a trial/court appearance or a bill coming due or a test coming up is absolutely worthless. Use your imagination to envision the best possible outcome instead.

If you pray, why worry and if you worry, why pray?

If you want further insights, please sign up for your complimentary Brilliance Breakthrough on my website www.CoachDeborah Downey.com and opt in to my newsletter and blog.

How to Manage Money and Invest Wisely

WHEN IT COMES to taking care of myself with money and credit cards and my spending needs, they all need to be practical, and at the same time, based in my spiritual beliefs. The idea of money is like energy and/or power. It allows or keeps me from doing things that I want to do. Yet it need not define me.

The energy it throws at us is neither good nor bad. Money and material things don't define our worth unless we decide that they do. We are all equally abundant if we are open to receive abundance. There is a difference between living with an abundant heart and feeling entitled, which carries with it a deep sense of anger and resentment and jealousy. Everyone can benefit from watching the film The Story of Stuff, which is at once so informative and also so scary. We all need to do our part. This film is so transformational in so many ways, it is a must-see for anyone with an over-spending problem.

The power of spending can get really, really addictive with credit card use. The best way to have control over your spending with a credit card is to use a debit card for day-to-day expenses, or use cash. For major purchases, either save up the cash to purchase the item or use your credit card, knowing and being prepared to pay it off in full every month. This will help you to live within your means, and it is important to live within your means and save for the future.

Pay yourself first every time you acquire any money or fees. Put ten percent of it into your personal savings and another five to ten percent away for gift-giving for the whole year. Keep track of your income and expenses on a weekly basis, if possible. When investing, check out the market and find comparables, and never take anything for granted. Verify every aspect of a company, a property, or a product. Read the fine print and look at product reviews. As with every other decision, always check in with your highest self, your spirit, or God, and ask for direction.

Don't let people insist that you act right away, this minute. If you do purchase anything impulsively, then don't be afraid to cancel the order and/or take something back. You have the right to change your mind. Please do so if you need to.

Money matters are always tricky in relationships with our parents, spouses, children, friends, and fellow workers. Life is not fair, so get over it. Some of the happiest people are what most Americans would declare as poor. My source of income and everything else is God, for all that I need, all that I have, all that I want, and it keeps me safe and away from what can harm me. When times are lean, never stop donating in your church or to charities, because you want the universe to know that you are abundant and you are acting accordingly.

I believe it is God's will for us all to live in abundance. Educate yourself and introduce your children to money matters. Show them what you do to manage your income and expenses. Teach your kids as much as you can about economics. Teach and model prudence, patience, and a positive approach to the use of money and saving. Only you can make yourself happy, sad, abundant, or poor. Your worth, however, is not contingent on how much cash or how many investments or assets you hold. Nothing you have is yours anyway to keep. It's all on loan from God.

How to Forgive Everybody Everything

I HIGHLY SUGGEST trying out a couple of these tips for shifts in your thinking.

Holding a person in contempt or worse, feeling hatred toward them, will always bring you more pain and waste your precious time much more than anything that they will ever feel or even be aware of. They may even know firsthand the extent of your dislike for them or their actions or attitudes and exactly what you dislike about them, or they may even realize how very opposite you both stand on any given issue. It doesn't matter because they more often than not don't care or remember what they did or did not do that made you angry. Here's the thing, though: I forgive a person not to give them relief. I forgive the person so I feel better. Period.

They can despise me all they need to because what other people think about me is none of my business. Whenever I'm upset, angry, or in fear, or feel victimized, or judge that I have been cheated or damaged, denied or deceived, there is something wrong with me, 99.9 percent of the time. I have put myself in a position to be hurt.

Now, I did not want to believe this at first, but my life experiences have proven to me over and over again that in the past, whenever I have been injured, I simply didn't take care of myself in a myriad of ways. Therefore, because I failed to protect myself, I had crappy consequences as a result of my sloth. I am guilty of being slothful when I don't ask questions or read the manual or read the directions, or when I don't do the background check, or I don't see and use experts in my area of decision-making.

One of the first questions I ask myself when I start feeling someone has harmed me is this: Is this forgivable? Now you may argue that murder is unforgivable, but history has shown lots of people who were able to forgive perpetrators of horrific acts of murder. I have not ever found anything that could not be forgiven because it is always my choice.

What is forgiveness, exactly? Forgiveness is, as it states in the dictionary, the act of excusing a mistake or offense. Mercy is the feeling that motivates compassion. Compassion generates the feelings that support the willingness to forgive. When we "pardon" and release someone from punishment and make them exempt from penalties, it does not mean that we cosign their bad behavior or agree with them or their attitudes or their beliefs. Forgiveness is not a free pass to do it again to me or to someone else.

When I have resentment against a person, a concept, or an institution, I have placed them on a hook, hanging for all to see. The trouble is that I am hanging on the hook right next to them. My life and my joy are stuck on that hook, and my creativity and usefulness to God and my fellows are frozen. Even though I have all the "time" I need, I don't want to spend my time strung up on that hook.

No person is perfect, and all of us have the same opportunity to follow negative thinking patterns of scarcity and hate each and every day. Just as easily we can choose healthy, kind, and loving and generous actions of the spirit, habits and mindsets that are compassionate and humble and generous of spirit.

When I forgive someone, I let them off the hook, but I do not forget what they did, nor do I forget how I put myself in that position with them to be mistreated. Perhaps I had an expectation of how they needed to perform something, or I simply assumed that they would know what I needed from them. I can't tell you how many times I got mad and disappointed when I felt someone failed me. As my years of taking stock of my thoughts and actions became a regular routine in my life, I saw clearly how many times I had not communicated what I wanted clearly and specifically. No one else is going to take better care of me than me. Other people don't always consider or even care what my needs are. Honestly, it is better if they don't anyway.

There is an air of superiority and control that often gets covered up when we forgive someone from our lofty position of forgiving them their sin against us. When I first get riled up at someone, I use this simple technique to get immediate relief. Then after I've cooled down, I do some quick writing to my Higher Power to sort through how I got myself in this mess.

So here is the quick solution: Go into a closet, usually secluded and private, or a quiet, secluded place, hopefully soundproof, like an insulated closet or shed, and assume the position, but never do this while driving the car. Collect some large pillows, then hit your knees and start pounding the pillows while yelling, "I forgive everybody everything!" Keep on pounding and screaming for as long as it takes to expel all the rage and until you are exhausted. Well, you may even start laughing. Laughing at my humanity and gullibility is the true sign of genius.

We give away our power to people whenever we hang on to old, worn-out injuries. Live in the now, forget the past, and plan to succeed in the future. It is so much more glorious than the past. The future will always be based and results will come from the attitudes and beliefs that I cultivate today.

Most folks are damaged, some more than others. We all get a bad day now and then. We all make mistakes. We all get seduced by our ego once in a while. I do not minimize or accept unkind, mean-spirited treatment from other people ever. I protect myself and always have a plan B ready. I do take responsibility for my actions, reactions, attitudes, and beliefs. I don't try to be like you, and I don't hold myself up to your standards.

When someone has made a mistake, I keep my distance until I see the light of atonement in their eyes. A genuine humility and a true willingness to repair, reconstruct, and to make a correction must be present from the offender before I get close to them again.

It is not what they say that shows me this change of heart in the offender. It is always what their actions bring forth. Until I see the shift in the person, I keep them at an arm's distance and do not leave myself open for attack.

When I harm someone and I'm not in denial about it, I ask the person how I can repair the damage I caused. I also can ask how I can make things right. I don't simply apologize. I have to do things differently.

In both cases, whether forgiving a person or making atonement to someone I have harmed, it is a spiritual matter. Either way, I pray for their highest good as well as mine. I ask for the right motive and timing and location from Spirit to make my amends to the person. My goal is to live happily each and every day with a true desire to serve God, my fellows, and myself. Since my serenity and well-being are on hold until I make things right with someone I have mistreated, I am anxious and enthusiastic to make my approach to the person. It is not important that they "forgive" me as God already has. I just really enjoy living with freedom. No amount of money or privilege can buy my freedom. I have also written letters to those I have harmed who have passed on. To the offender or the victim of my mistakes, my letters can release them and bless them. Direct face-to-face amends are better than letters to those I have offended, but when the only option is a letter, I always can ask them to release me from their contempt and guide me to the right actions to take to make amends to them.

It is always important to get clarity about what you are making the amends for and why. You are not auditioning for love or acceptance; those you get from God. I make amends to repair things. I forgive to release my suffering and get off the hook that has me captive.

How to Identify if You Are Operating from Out-Dated Ideas that Came from Your Parents or Your Childhood! Are You Missing Something?

OKAY, PLEASE UNDERSTAND. My intention is not to reopen old wounds and ruminate on our parents or other caregivers' mistakes so we can then blame and/or seek revenge. I am suggesting that as an adult, we will benefit from looking at our current beliefs to see if they are ours or are they in fact our parents. Do your attitudes and standards truly reflect who you want to be? I ask you, my readers, to question everything you think you believe and ask yourselves, "Is this working for me? Am I happy with my results?"

For the purpose of this book and the reader's personal growth, my definition of dysfunctional is a parent or guardian's unloving and dominating behaviors, language and messages to their children. Do most of their communications carry a non-constructive perspective and a level of shaming criticism and undermining amount of sheer control? Most people have parents who make mistakes now and then out of fear. Even if our parents did love us and did take time to guide and teach us and also did protect us and try to nurture us, does it mean we did not suffer growing up, and that we did internalize ideas and attitudes of a sick, shame-based family member that we cling to? The good news is we are not stuck with their standards and fear-based mode of reacting to life. We may not change the past, but by looking back we can change our future. We have the right to grow past what our parents' generations used for its standards and rules.

Listen, I do not wish to attack anyone's parents by writing about this. I had alcoholic parents whom I loved deeply and am very grateful that I got them as my parents. They did the best they knew how. The last five to ten years of their lives, I had very warm and loving relationships with them based on admiration and respect. I even had the opportunity to pray with them on a very intimate basis, something we never did while I was a child except for saying "Grace" before dinner once in a while. My mother and father were funny and playful and smart and stylish, but they were also misguided in many ways and had prejudices and behaviors that were toxic. I absorbed everything, and it took me a good fifteen years to sort through it all and find out what really worked for me. I know I am not alone here.

Adult children of either alcoholic or dysfunctional parents develop poor life skills as a direct response to the lack of healthy parenting they received growing up. As children, there was no protection or escape from our parents. If we had to endure life at the mercy of their physical, emotional, financial, and spiritual sickness, well, we were damaged. We had to find a way, healthy or not, to survive the episodes of abandonment or abuse, mentally and/or physically, we were subjected to.

I consider myself an expert in this niche because I have been diligently looking and recovering from my own erroneous survivor traits for the all these years without any time out. I have helped my clients discover their bad habits and reframe their damaged ideas and coping skills and attitudes, and helped them to gain clarity and regain their lost power of choice. Yes, it's true; we had lame habits and bad attitudes. We need to create new habits and new attitudes that enhance and truly support our life goals. Believe me, I know it is scary to look back. I felt numb to the growing possibility that my parents' behavior while I was a child had so deeply wounded me. I must move past the message that society and the media tells me. The message they shout is "Get Over It!" Thanks, I'd love to but how can I? How do I forget and move forward, when I barely recognize that I have been bleeding and allowing tormentors to stomp on my soul for the last ten years?

There is no use to remaining in denial; this work cannot be

ignored, as it is the final frontier for those of us seeking our maximum potential during our life on this planet. Not only is this deep work needed to fully live a well-traveled existence; it is also a must for spiritual growth. Make no mistake, this self-reflection and review of family events is not a quick fix. Constant awareness is required to get the clarity needed to change our paradigm…thoroughness pays big rewards on the journey to self-love and life mastery.

During my process, I got really connected to my core feelings and gained a much more intimate relationship to my Creator, my Higher Power.

I have seen my clients benefit immensely after very little exposure to this type of work. Unfortunately, without continued work in this area, the majority of my fellow travelers will relapse back to their dysfunctional ways. You may ask, "What is an ACA relapse?" Well, trying to control everybody is a huge red flag. Relapse occurs when any kind of acting out takes place and serves as a clue that you're slipping backward into adult child behavior. I call this kind of reckless behavior following "the Call of the Wild." It includes keeping secrets, people-pleasing, being dishonest with yourself, and/or being self-indulgent.

The disease is so sneaky, it often lies dormant for years. If an adult child's behavior remains undiscovered and shoved under the carpet, experience has proven to me that the adult child will unwittingly make self-harming choices, not understanding why or how they could keep doing the same mistakes again and again. Recognizing that the main influences of our thinking and attitudes, habits and actions, come from our formative years saves the adult child much heartache and suffering. Unfortunately, these hidden impulses and these early messages, if left covered up and locked away in our minds, will undermine our lives continually. Our only hope is to stay one step ahead of our ego and its effort to pull us down. With practice, one can pull the thread of today's actions and outcomes and find the negative, unhealthy event that coaxed us to go in this direction. This awareness of our patterns alone gives us back our freedom of choice to accept or reject an idea or a plan before any action is taken on our part. We really can redesign our lives and acquire our hearts' desires when we make good decisions based on our highest good. I have had to re-parent myself and forgive myself for the things I did before gaining the insights that this work, this self-reflection, continues to reveal to me.

I lived so much of my life in an unconscious state. I call it "bumper car existence"—random, and at the same time, repetitive living, as I made the same poor choices over and over again. I was unable to see that I kept falling into the same hole on the same road. I tried to jump the hole, and I fell in, and then I tried to sidestep the hole, and fell in, and then I tried to skirt by the hole from both sides, and fell in. Each time, convinced I was doing something differently.

After some time learning about how my mind had been negatively conditioned, it occurred to me I was free for the first time to consider using a different road. What an idea!

After several more years of recovery, I realized that I could take even better care of myself by comparing and choosing the best road possible on an as-needed basis. I even gave myself permission to change my mind and change my plans as often as I felt the need. I learned to honor my intuitive self and honor the universe at the same time.

To recap, if your parents were unloving and mean to you—it doesn't matter if they were alcoholics, addicts, crazy, controlling, abandoned you, abusive to you, were overly strict, were overly protective, or were overly permissive—you have been deeply impacted by your upbringing and learned coping skills to save your life and sanity that probably don't serve you. You've been damaged, whether you want to admit it or not. You are not alone.

I have met and coached several groups of men and women who were raised by parents who lacked healthy parenting techniques and modeled or spoke negatively to their kids. If you had that kind of a parent, or perhaps a guardian or older sibling, you are more than likely living your adult life severely disturbed and at the mercy of your survival traits. This is perhaps why, despite your best efforts, you find yourself a failure in love relationships or with money matters. Your core belief about yourself, whether conscious or not, is that you are worthless. You can take every seminar and seek multiple teachers, mentors, and gurus, but unless you do some work facing and gaining clarity about the damage you suffered growing up, even if you survived your suffering, you will forever be doomed to recreate the recurring events and actions and the ensuing, habitual pain you had as a kid.

Dealing with the sense of shame and your inherent feelings of being a victim will cause you to put yourself in positions to be hurt like you were in the past. This allows you to return to the familiar feelings of your childhood reality. Alas, so even if you think you've moved on or perhaps even forgiven the people who were the original offenders, you must take continuous, consistent steps to re-parent yourself and overcome the post-traumatic stress you endured. Otherwise, if you don't, you will find yourself reliving similar events, if not the exact events! Finding true love is impossible unless and until you find peace within your family of origin. In fact, in an effort to heal my past, I married a man just like my unavailable, emotional and physically abandoning father. I next married someone just as controlling and narcissistic as my mother often was when I was growing up. I became engaged to marry another man who had low self-esteem, who was an addict and bipolar, and who was mildly effeminate, like my beautiful, gay brother. My third husband was just like me, and our union seemed perfect because we had so much in common. For one, we both needed the spotlight and adoring fans. Turned out our real attraction was that we shared common childhood wounds and survival traits. Neither one of us could help the other.

Growing up in chaos and danger lays the groundwork for an adult life of uncertainty and the unspoken need to be on guard. The by-product of this environment is an inability to make mature, informed decisions in a timely manner. The number one need for an adult child is the compulsion to control nearly everything possible. Our work atmosphere, our home environment, our loved ones are all the subjects of our need to be in control. No one likes to be controlled, and it is especially true of our lovers and mates. The need to change and control our spouses is the most common complaint of couples in divorce proceedings. Here again, the desire for control is not obvious to most adult children. They don't recognize that they are controlling and see themselves as being helpful and caring. If and when enough of their friends and family members challenge them and protest about the constant control they are facing, does the adult child's defenses lower enough for them to grasp their control issues. For some wounded adult children, the opposite of needing control manifests as living in a magical, fantasy mindset, leaving these individuals in a completely vulnerable position to be cheated or stolen from or taken advantage of. These people do not take care of themselves. They refuse to read the instructions, or read the small print, and refuse to look closely at the details or do research before signing on the dotted line. Understandably, these adult children are perpetually set up to be victims and live their lives in major self-pity, anger, and blame. These people give away their power to others routinely. My awareness shifted from denial to anger after several months of sobriety, when I finally could see and digest the extent of the control and manipulation my parents had had over me.

My mentor encouraged me to feel my anger and write about it and refrain from my tendency to minimize events. My mother particularly had controlled me with money and the threat to deny me access to money and an inheritance. Her money was a leash that kept me around. My drinking had been a way to rebel and punish my parents for their domination and the lies they'd fed me while I was growing up. For six months or so, I distanced myself from my parents until I could acquire some balance from my previous denial and newly embraced anger. Those closest to me were the ones who got the brunt of my newfound awareness.

I would swing from being a people-pleaser to downright defiance with twenty minutes, when I felt someone was bossing me around. The first ten months of my sobriety, I faced panic attacks nearly every morning. I came to understand that these attacks were typical of children of alcoholics and addicts and dysfunctional parents. My own drinking had started out as a way to self-medicate and initially had been a reprieve, if you will, for my daily frustrations with control and unspoken fears. My drinking's progression had turned my escape into an additional burden that added to my overwhelming guilt and low self-esteem.

I always suggest that adult children from dysfunctional homes attain abstinence from any addiction and maintain their recovery for a minimum of three years before delving into any of this deep adult child work, because this work brings new awareness, and the feelings this new insight stirs up can trigger relapse back into their addiction. Before I could really rebuild my self-worth, I had to take responsibility for my own alcoholism, and have and maintain a rigorous program of recovery. It was after eight years of solid sobriety that my formal adult child recovery work began. This healing journey is different from any other recovery process.

This recovery is nonlinear and often erratic, and one can take a giant step forward, yet follow up soon after with two steps backwards. Understanding we have choices and can choose new beliefs and try out new behaviors is often a slow and seeming impossible undertaking. The key for this kind of work to succeed is to stay engaged, such as by working with a coach or joining a group, and by reading about this work on a weekly basis.

My discovery process has been a slow unveiling of defective thinking and destructive habits and behaviors. Developing a willingness to try new approaches, often on blind faith and being okay with failing now and then, can take some time for us to integrate. Granting yourself permission to proceed is an individual decision to make and merits large amounts of self-praise. It also helps to find like-minded travelers to encourage this work and keep us accountable.

I personally continue with my recovery process even though both my parents and my only sibling have passed on. I lead groups and have phone meetings and read various materials on the subject to retain and further my awareness and new insights so I can get better, plus be ready to share my recovery and deep understanding of the journey with my clients and help my fellow travelers avoid pitfalls that I was able to avoid myself. I have proven techniques and a five-step system of recovery I use to facilitate this journey. I can testify that before each of my family members walked on…I had come to peace with them, found forgiveness, and had nothing but love and gratitude toward them. I was free of shame, guilt, and anger. Today, I am happily married and at peace with my three grown children and my three step-children. I love my Higher Power and myself unconditionally and no longer seek or demand approval from outside of myself. My life works and I enjoy it! Please go to: wwwCoachDeborahDowney.com

Sign up for your **Complimentary Brilliance Breakthrough Session!**

How to Ignite Your Inner Child's Love for You

WITHIN EACH OF us, there are stored memories and core values and accumulated life templates. Most people have good and bad experiences that they were forced to endure from adults in their lives when they were children. The adults could've been parents, older siblings, grandparents, teachers, preachers, doctors, law enforcement, or government agencies. The small percent of people without any interaction with adults would have to consider the oldest child present in their life as the adult figure. Regardless of the characters and the actions and behaviors, all these "adults" impacted us when we were dependent and essentially captive and powerless and naïve as children. We developed coping traits and mindsets and behaviors to survive and protect our lives. The possibilities are endless when it comes to our coping and our inner dialogue and our hopes, as a result.

I feel that no matter how loving or hateful these interactions were, they were internalized messages that we began hearing, and they came to dictate our actions, and will continue to run the show unless we look back and name it, claim it, and determine if we want it anymore, or if we want to dump it.

Once I began looking back at photos and started probing and remembering, I started to regain my personal power, because now I was awake, and I knew what I wanted. Now, today, I know what I want. I began by finding a photo of myself as a seven-year-old with my German shepherd. Smoothie was his name. I took this photo and found another photo of my adult self, and cut out the other person's torso, and put the two photos, me as a child and me as an adult, together. My outstretched arm wrapped perfectly around my younger self. I framed this combination photo and began remembering a lot of my childhood.

Then I made a child box. I found a heart-shaped Valentine, flocked box and put in as many childhood treasures as I could find. I included my report cards and a pin from a singing competition I had won. I put in a newspaper article about me as a child. I added my own children's and my grandchildren's photos, and all my pets' pictures, and I put my husband's—pictures of them as a child. Some candy I used to love to eat. I put in little treasures that I had—feathers and jewelry and such. I encourage people to make their own child box. Find a photo of yourself as a little person that you love and create your own child box. I write letters to my younger self, and she writes back to me. I write my childhood prayers. I use colors and toys to decorate a small space in my house. I look at these things a couple of times a year. I don't need to share or show these private things to anyone unless I want to, but it's nice to know, and it opens the dialogue between me and my younger self, and we become united.

How to Identify Your Defective Thoughts and Attitudes
Their Definitions

DEFECTIVE THOUGHTS AND poor attitudes that arise when I slip into my lower self and my ego are the things that make my mind troubled. Here is a brief description of each of the ones that I have identified that get in my way, and I find are pretty universal:

1. The first one is **giving away my power.** This is when we let someone else's opinion of us define us and give away our power. It is giving my self-worth, happiness, self-esteem to a person instead of trusting my own and my Higher Power's standards as my guide.

2. The next one is **anger**. Anger is holding ill feelings, condemning, wanting to punish, or to lash back at some person, place, or thing.

3. **Beating myself up.** This is an unpleasant form of self-obsession and self-hatred, a form of shame and impatience.

4. **Rage** is extreme anger, a form of a trance which propels violent language and actions.

5. **Projection** is thinking ahead and imagining the many potentially dangerous, unpleasant outcomes.

6. **Intolerance.** This is acute judgment and comparison, an easy way to separate myself from others and feel better than, special, and superior.

7. **Remorse.** The negative process of looking back in my unhealthy past and keep reliving and revisiting an old defect.

8. **Apathy.** The highest form of self-pity and laziness.

9. **Pride.** Mindless entitlement, driven by generational hate and need to intimidate others.

10. **Obsession.** It's a train of negative thoughts that push away all logic and self-love.

11. **Perfectionism.** An uncanny, insane drive to do more than possible, which is a complete form of self-absorption.

12. **Keeper of the justice.** This is a belief that my way is the right way, and others must follow my plans. This is an unconscious habit of comparison and the need to order others to adhere to my plan or standards of conduct.

13. **Arrogance.** This is forgetting my experiences and culture and environment, and therefore my needs are all different from other people. The idea that my way is the right way, or worse, it's the only way. This is the height of stupidity or terrorism.

14. **Self-pity.** Classic self-absorption and sinking into the memories of the past (or future) while being disconnected to the present. Feeling that I am being picked on—that everything is out to get me.

15. **Lustful.** Imagining sexual thoughts or needing conquest devoid of love or reciprocity, and/or any form of responsibility or commitment to the person of our attention.

16. **Selfishness.** Considering only my needs or wants.

17. **Self-centeredness.** Taking anything that happens as solely about me.

18. **Self-absorption.** A complete lack of awareness of others; an insatiable desire for attention from other people.

19. **Expectation.** When I have a predetermined outcome for someone else's behavior or thoughts.

20. **People-pleasing.** This is a cunning, dishonest action or thought to get or maintain approval. Lying to others so I can seem deserving of their approval at the expense of my personal truth.

21. **Low self-esteem.** A bewildered and weak view of my personal worth, plus no ability to feel valuable and intelligent or possessing any important skill set.

22. **Shame.** This is the feeling of deep loss of self because I don't measure up, and my efforts have failed. Often feelings of false responsibility toward close relationships.

23. **Guilt** is reflecting on mistakes in the past—a way to justify not doing what I promised to do.

24. **Sloth.** This is self-sabotage in the extreme. Silent protests from my abandoned inner child. A low-level form of contempt for others. Feelings of overwhelm and making decisions without checking in with God.

25. **Envy.** Wanting what someone else possesses. Comparing and feeling unable to rise up to the challenges of life.

26. **Greed.** To have everything you've always wanted, yet to claim what is yours and still demand more, or someone else's.

27. **Jealousy.** People who are petty and pretty dissatisfied. This is a compliment to the person, in a weird way, but leaves you feeling left in the cold.

28. **Control.** This is a false sense of power—the need to organize, save, or fix others.

29. **Gluttony.** The desire to have more once I have gotten my portion. An obsession to get more of everything. Self-care has been eclipsed by greed.

How to Let Go of Defective Thoughts and Behaviors
My Simple Process for Removing Defective Thoughts, and Two Techniques for Calming My Mind Before I Sleep

ALL RIGHT. So I defined several harmful ideas and attitudes. So here is my simple process for letting go of the egocentric thoughts, attitudes, and accompanying actions and reactions that stand in the way of my happiness. I defined these defects of thought and attitudes, so now I want to share with you how I let them go.

I write a letter to my Source when I find myself stuck in a nonproductive mindset, and feeling irritable and depressed. If I'm feeling like that more than fifteen minutes, I know it's time to write this letter. And the letter goes something like: "Dear Higher Power," and then I give Him or Her or It all of my resentments, fears, thoughts, anger, resentment, rage... I put it all on paper. I hold nothing back. I get down and dirty and I say whatever I need to say, and I don't censor it. I get petty.

And then at the very end, I surrender. I say, "I can't do this alone. Please help me. Please remove these things that are standing in my way and help me find a way to do your will," and then I sign my name.

And then I go back and I revisit it. I look at it. I look at what I've written, and I find where I have these thoughts that are defective, and I list them on the margin. And then at the end, once I have a clear vision of my powerlessness and my perfectionism and my beating myself up, and my anger, and my resentment, and my keeper of the justice, whatever I have listed there, I then ask God to remove it.

Now I can suffer as long or as little as I want, because my happiness and serenity are my responsibility.

My life today looks and feels exactly the way I determine it to look today. I'm not a hostage or a victim anymore. No longer do I hold on to my problems or fears, and no longer do I try to fix yours or help you fix yours. If I find myself unhappy or in fear or bored, I know I have to either change my thinking and attitudes and write a letter and ask God to help me, or I need to take an action, either towards some goal I want or some person that I want to approach, or it may mean that I need to remove myself from a situation or a person and stop seeing them and putting myself in a position to be hurt.

So if I need help with taking an action that I find scary or difficult, I first check with myself to see what is motivating my desire to do this. Is the motive healthy? And is it self-nurturing? If it is, then I go ahead and I proceed with as big a step towards what I want to do as I'm comfortable with. If it's not self-nurturing and coming from my self-esteem and love and belief in myself, then I know I shouldn't do it.

Sometimes, though, what I want to do is something I need to do, and I don't like to do it. It could be doing my taxes or writing a letter to someone I don't want to write to. And whatever those cases are, then I have to employ my personal discipline. I do that by setting a timer, a minute timer for forty-five minutes, and I sit down for that forty-five minutes, and I do the task until the buzzer goes off. At that point, I take a break and do a few errands or whatever I need to do, and then if I come back and I have the energy and the time, I'll set the timer for another forty-five-minute session.

Another technique I have to calm my nerves is, upon going to bed, I will review my day and note the things that I did well, and also the things that I want to improve. But if I find that I'm thinking about stuff, and I'm worrying about certain things and outcomes and people and institutions, whatever, I'll put them on a piece of paper. I'll list them, and I'll put that list at the foot of the bed, and I'll ask God to give me the solutions the following day. And then I will expect to see them, and they will come: in the newspaper, or someone will say something to me, or I'll read it somewhere, or it'll be on TV. I expect a miracle. I expect the answer. And it comes.

The other thing I do at night is a simple prayer. Because I had my own share of religious residue, I didn't want to just say prayers from rote, so I decided to write my own. And my prayer goes like this:

> *Dear God,*
> *Please put me where you'd have me be. Doing what you'd have me do. Seeing what you'd have me see. Thinking what you'd have me think. Feeling what you'd have me feel. Please help me to be of service and of value to you, my fellows, and myself. May I do your will always.*
> *Love,*
> *Deborah*

How to Stop Smoking

My experience of how I quit smoking will also apply to other bad habits. Like lots of people, I started smoking at a fairly young age. I tried all sorts of ways to stop, but lacked "willpower" and allowed myself to believe that if I was angry, then I could give myself permission to settle my nerves with a cigarette or two. The trouble was, I was angry a lot when I was young.

I also was unaware that once I satisfied my craving by smoking, my body really craved more, so controlled smoking by cutting back to fewer and fewer cigarettes never accomplished my goal of being a nonsmoker. As well as a physical stimulant and nerve-calmer, nicotine and the social behaviors associated with smoking cigarettes had become part of my personal style. Fortunately, the media and my children and all of the negative comments and the growing awareness of the many hazards associated with cigarette smoking squelched the romantic and any remnants of glamour concerning smoking. They were eclipsed, and any and all positive benefits I had kept on justifying the habit with finally sunk in.

Finally, I could clearly see and admit I was a hypocrite, and could no longer fool myself. I quit smoking once and for all fifteen years ago, cold turkey. I decided that I would not give myself permission to smoke ever again. I realized that making this decision not to smoke, no matter what, was the main ingredient I needed to succeed. My decision was made without any reservation or exceptions, save one. I asked my Higher Power every morning to take away my obsession to smoke cigarettes, and I agreed that I would not purchase any cigarettes, or steal any, or bum any cigarettes, every day for thirty days. Then I re-upped to sixty days. Then ninety days, and so on. I am now smoke-free for over fifteen years.

I chewed gum, drank lots of water, ate fruits to diminish the physical cravings. I did tell God if a cigarette floated into my mouth that I would smoke it, but that's never happened.

I did attend a Smokers Anonymous meeting about a year before I actually ultimately quit smoking. It was in Smokers Anonymous that I learned that my cravings would subside within minutes, whether I satisfied them by smoking or not. So I asked God to help me resist cravings if they came up, and they rarely did.

Oddly enough, though, about eighteen months into my recovery from this addiction, while driving on the L.A. freeways, I saw a passing vehicle with a man smoking. And somehow, it triggered me momentarily. Then I said a prayer, and I asked God to remind me of our agreement. Earlier, I called myself a hypocrite because I knew that I had been asking God to cure my M.S.—my multiple sclerosis—while I had continued to abuse my nervous system by sucking down nicotine.

Some of the other things that I did to help myself were:

1. I changed the places I went.

2. I avoided hanging out with smokers.

3. I began eating better—less salty foods and less sugary foods.

4. Lastly, I stopped drinking sodas and drinking alcohol.

The key for my abstinence was not contingent on whether other people I loved or was friends with smoked or didn't. This was a big help, because my husband at the time did smoke, and a large part of our eight-month courtship had been sitting on a couch in my apartment in Playa del Rey, smoking and chatting. He had no desire to quit, and actually added cigars into his smoking repertoire. He never stopped, and died of a heart attack in 2007, two days after finding out he was diagnosed with lung cancer.

I did not hound him to quit, but did ask him not to smoke in our home or in my car. It never became an issue for us. I expressed my fears and concerns about his smoking once, and after that, said nothing, except when he would light up in my car. I knew it would be the start of a fight, but I was not going to back down. I learned to drive myself a lot, and was nonjudgmental, and I didn't act superior in any way. I spoke my truth once, and he told me where he stood. And I said nothing more.

I will say I was angry at his obsession and fanatical addiction to his smoking habit. When I was cleaning out our storage rental compartment, I found a large box overloaded with empty cigar boxes—small and large, fancy and plain—also, two humidifiers and cigar ashtrays, and a couple of cigar cutters. He had had a shrine in our home in Half Moon Bay in his office to his true first love—cigars and cigarettes. And I was angry about that. But then I remembered that he had the right to be wrong. When I say wrong, I mean by my standards. I mean wrong for me. I share my feelings here in the hope that what I reveal may impact a smoker or two. But he did have the right to smoke. It was his body and his right.

I realized that I had been in a three-way relationship. He would leave me at the stroke of midnight of New Year's Eve to steal away to smoke, or he would abandon me at a restaurant to sit by myself for ten to fifteen minutes for his return while he would enjoy his passion for nicotine. I had work to do after his passing. My reaction after this was, well, I was shocked by his sudden death, and after much writing and looking at my part, I came to accept that it was his decision, and my reaction was more of gratitude that I had made my decision to quit. By making up my mind and changing my habits and friends, I had set myself free. Smokers are never in the now. They are in a state of anticipation, waiting for their fix.

I do believe I could not have quit without God's help. I could love the man and still hate his addiction. His addiction stole his life and many precious moments of our time together, but addiction is not a moral weakness or a personal flaw. I have been able to forgive myself for my anger at his passing, and I have found serenity knowing we all have our own path and our own consequences to face. With addiction comes a certain amount of insanity, or even arrogance, that all the fears and warnings of continued usage don't apply to them, or to me. My husband's best friend had died a slow death from lung cancer. It never fazed him.

I only need follow my truth. They follow theirs. My father, mother, and only brother all suffered health problems due to smoking. For some obtuse reason, I was given the strength and the desire to stop. God gave me the grace to do it. And I am eternally in His debt.

How to Find Your Loving Higher Power

Please keep your mind open to embracing your own personal Higher Power or God or Goddess or Spirit or Great Intelligence. Using a Higher Power as your partner in life will only advance your life experiences, and I don't think people who refuse to believe in God are belligerent or arrogant, as many believers may assert. Rather, I think that nonbelievers get stuck because they're judging the ways and the motives of the believers, and they see them as self-serving people who need to control others from their lofty spiritual, superior stance.

God has been given a bad name because of the atrocities, intolerance, and actions, and overbearing, self-important attitudes and supercilious airs certain religious men and women have presented throughout history. But this is not God's way. It is the ego's path.

Believing and using a connection to a Higher Power or God of your design is uplifting. It's not a cop-out or an admission of weakness or stupidity. The surrender to asking for inspiration and direction from God is at once empowering. Believing in God or Goddess will never erase or minimize your unique, humorous, irreverent personality, or mine.

I've known lots of people over the years who had off-the-wall humor and outrageous personalities and definitely swore up a blue streak, and even they were able to find a power greater than themselves that they could turn to and they could accept and incorporate into their lives. I suggest just writing your own personal ad to request your ideal and instantly available Higher Power to apply for this ongoing, non-paying position. It can go something like this: "Wanted: Some kind, all-knowing, all-powerful Higher Power. Please, no shamers or blamers need apply. Must have a great sense of humor, and complete willingness to show up and problem-solve, but only when asked. Must be fun and not too needy or too judgmental or controlling." So you see, the possibilities and the specifications are endless. You can ask anything you want. It's unlimited.

Scientists like Einstein and learned people all over the country and throughout history have believed and benefitted from adding and letting God into their plans and endeavors and discoveries. Just forget all of the negative press and tragedies that have been attributed to clergy and the sick people who have performed atrocities in God's name. We all have free will; my life works best when I align my will with God's will.

So what is God's will, and how do you know what it is, and what's the difference? Well, I consider God's will to feel like this: God's will is effortless and easy. God's will rings clear as a bell. God's will is what is happening. God's will feels right. It feels good. And so that means everything else must be my ego.

So that means when things don't feel good or work easily, and I get stressed or I'm confused or I'm in misery, I'm in my ego. Now, as I align my will with my Higher Power's will, I simply relax and can stop trying to figure things out or fix things, people, and myself. And then I find peace of mind. God will only perform solutions for me for my life if I let Him. Spirit does not go where it has not been invited.

To be sure, if my gut is in a knot, and I feel confused and angry or fearful, I'm in my will, not God's. And if I resist God's will, I suffer.

The spiritual path does not promise that I won't come up against problems or disaster, only that I will be given the tools and the best attitude to take care of myself as I walk through the rocky or unwanted, unfavorable misfortunes I face. So even when I'm unhappy and I can't see any good or any positive outcome, I may still hold tightly to what I have come to call "God." I can celebrate and praise God anywhere as often as possible, as often as I need.

The remainder of this book is to basically train and enlighten you on how to cultivate and streamline your inward journey to your Higher Power. And once you begin to see this power, I can start showing you practical practices you can apply each day of your life that will ultimately restore you to health, wealth, and peace of mind. God is my source, my protector, my advisor, my employer, my love, my friend. I feel relief when I remind myself that God is my source. I am free of my ego, my personal prosecuting attorney, and punishing, unforgiving, unforgetting tormentor. I fire my ego every morning, and my attitude and my thinking and behaviors are elevated to a higher plane.

So I suggest whenever you're stressed, or feeling angry, that you try this little exercise that I came up with. And it goes like this: Because I work for and trust in God, _____. So you can write sentences like that. Because I work for and trust in God, fill in the blank. I'll give you some examples.

《 Because I work for and trust in God, I listen with compassion to others and my intuitive voice within.

《 Because I trust in God and work for God, I am courageous and learn new things, and can stand up to abusive people in a kind and forgiving way.

《 Because I work for and I trust in God, I sleep soundly and wake with joy and energy.

《 Because I work for and trust in God, I enjoy peace of mind with all my family and dear friends, and all my associates and tenants.

《 Because I work for and trust in God, I am loved and liked and valued by all.

That's just an example. May I assume if you continue to read this book, you are considering at least to try out, or you're already enjoying, a Higher Power daily. But if you just try it for a week or so, you'll have an idea. So that said, here's a phrase that I tell myself once or twice a week at least. It goes like this: God gives me what I need to know on a need-to-know basis. Don't you love that?

I think it's amazing, because if my ego, which I call Shirley Temptress, wants to razz me or sabotage my efforts, I can just turn her off, and walk away and do something else, or try calling someone to be of service to them to change the energy that's blocking in the air. Now, I don't have to force the solution. I don't have to know everything. I can turn my attention to helping or calling someone I know whom I might be able to praise or uplift.

The Best and Most Considerate Way to Treat Physically or Mentally Handicapped People

BEFORE I BECAME afflicted with multiple sclerosis, I generally pitied and avoided people stricken by disabling diseases and those people disfigured by events or people born without the typical features known to the majority of people around the globe.

I attribute my judgments and need to be separate and somehow better than these people as the result of fear, plain and simple. Add in the odd notion that I might in some strange way actually catch what had made them that way made my attitude worse. Honestly, in my ignorance, I was also scared by people who were different, scarred, misshapen from birth. I even have witnessed people recoil from older people, folks with similar discomfort.

All this changed once I was diagnosed with multiple sclerosis. My first reaction when I was diagnosed was that of anger and self-pity. Why me? And also a low-grade form of shame. I was damaged goods, and my parents' refusal to accept the diagnosis aggravated my grief and gave my ego lots of fuel to try and run my show. Fortunately, I was newly sober, all of two months, when I found out that I was officially diagnosed with multiple sclerosis. I had gone to four previous doctors over the past year and a half, and they had all uniformly said I might have MS. My wobbly gait had become obvious enough that people were mentioning it now often.

Over the last twenty-five years, I have come to appreciate the many gifts I have received and continue to receive from this distinction as a handicapped person with special needs. I now am in the minority class vocation, just like people of color and also people of non-Christian faith are the minority.

I had to learn how to advocate for myself as well as many other learning character-building techniques. Here is the list, a handy list, of guidelines. I like to suggest these to dispel fear and the need to separate myself from others.

1. Kindness is the best gift I can give my fellows and myself.

2. Humility. Remembering to stay in gratitude and not compare or compete.

3. Always ask if you can be of assistance to anyone who is handicapped. Never assume the person needs or wants assistance.

4. Disability does not mean inferiority or that they are dim-witted or unlucky or that their condition is their fault.

5. Do visit handicapped people often.

6. Open doors and in general be courteous to handicapped people.

7. Be genuine and respectful of handicapped people.

8. Take gifts and offer to be of service often. Everyone likes a present.

9. Don't offer unsolicited advice, opinions, or direction.

10. Don't have fear about their condition and constantly share it with them. Handicapped people have their own fears to contend with. Don't bring up their past mistakes or tell them how they are being punished for their mistakes by their handicap disease.

11. Don't avoid contact with any handicapped person because you feel guilty that you are whole and see them as not.

12. Don't ask insulting questions. An example would be when I'm at an event and someone comes up and asks me if I can drive. Seems pretty apparent I got there.

13. Don't ask a handicapped person if they need your help constantly.

14. Don't infantilize them in any way.

15. Don't underrate or overrate their ability to take care of themselves.

16. Don't enable them to over-medicate or to try to relinquish their abilities for self-care in any way or any area of their lives.

17. Don't act or speak to a handicapped person without thinking, "Is this respectful and generous of spirit and loving?"

18. Don't express your disappointment, fears, anger, and frustration about their predicament with them. Process your feelings with someone else.

19. Don't shame or blame them or other people or circumstances or God for their disease. Instead, gratitude, love, and encouragement and faith and hope are the gifts you can sprinkle on them daily.

Reaffirming how special and incredible they are daily creates an atmosphere where miracles occur. You can even be another miracle in their lives as well. We all surrender inevitably as we grow older. Handicapped people have a head start, and hold many keys to our personal success, all of us.

I no longer ask, "Why me?" I say thank you and ask, "How can I be of service?" I try to love handicapped people and people that don't understand, and may be toxic. I try to love them anyway. I'm so grateful to know and feel that I am blessed and have so much to give to all people as a result of my multiple sclerosis. I am no longer separate, and I embrace everyone I meet. Some individuals and/or cultures and/or governments are toxic, and they're misguided, so I love them in a very special way—from an arm's distance.

III. Family, Children, and Divorce

Parenting: A Higher Calling

MEN AND WOMEN with children especially have very special challenges and very little time or opportunity to take care, to help
others, to pray, or to call a friend. No, to these young people, I say,
"Just breathe, and praise your child for every little positive thing
they do." I think being a parent is a sacred and beautiful honor. I
believe that we actually choose our parents, so our kids picked us,
and learning how to say no to my children from my assets, which
are honesty, self-love, protection, and for my love, is the key that
I've found to hold myself in balance.

If I say no from anger or control or a power position, or from
my neurotic fears, then my children will not comply, and the battle
of wills will ensue. Rest and diet are huge factors for parents as
much as the baby, the child, or the teenager. None of us does very
well without enough rest.

Children's naps are a gift to them as well as Mom and Dad,
and my three children had two naps a day until they were three,
and then they had long naps at three o'clock in the afternoon until
they were five. Looking back, I wish I had had less outings and
activities and more quiet time reading or baking or gardening. I say
this because I do think children today, especially, get conditioned
to need constant outside stimulation. Well, I find that the opposite

is also dangerous; isolation and never getting any socialization is not good, either, because children need new experiences to grow and know how to be in society.

Children need structure and routine and chores and lots of praise and attention. Finding ways to trade with other families to share the care for the little ones is a great help for moms and dads, who can also take turns with the kids. When my children got older and they would be pushing me to let them go somewhere, I learned to say, "Hmm. I'll think about it. If I have to answer right away, then my answer is no. But if I can let you know tomorrow, well, I might say yes."

When my children grew up, I did not give unsolicited advice, especially when they were telling me their plans and ideas. One of my mentors taught me to say, "Hmm. That's very interesting," and then ask, "Would you care for some feedback?" Sometimes, my children would say yes, and sometimes they'd say no. Either way, it was okay.

On occasion, one of my children would ask me for my opinion on something concerning their partners or personal matters. When I'm invited to comment, I consider how this might have repercussions, and often will say something like, "I have no comment. I don't know. I don't have any input." Because I never want to hand anyone the silver bullet to shoot me with later, when they are, of course, now mad at me, or are back together with their partner.

No, my children are quite brilliant, and in fact, my kids have all been my teachers from time to time, and continue to influence my personal growth. Accepting that I do not own my children allows me to love them in a detached, yet truly healthy, loving way. My child is on loan from God. I have the honor to care for and protect and sustain them with food, shelter, and education.

My philosophy is that I set limits for my children to ensure their safety and well-being. I like to think of these limits that I set as kind of an expanding playpen, which continues to get larger and bigger until it has become like a lovely, white picket corral that, eventually, I must leave open. Because if I keep it shut, and I lock it, my child will jump it, usually too early. My experience is that the more I try to clutch my children, the more likely I will cripple them, much like grabbing onto a butterfly, or trying to help open the cocoon of the emerging butterfly.

I love the poet David Whyte's thoughts on young girls needing to explore their own mysteries and find their own true voice and passions. Showing my children that I can take care of myself, I believe, is the highest spiritual lesson I can model for them. I know ultimately, we will all die, and no one can help us to avoid it or postpone it. My true purpose is to live until I die. To live fully, and to make no one else responsible for my choices, is liberating for me, undoubtedly, but also for everyone else in my life.

Loving my children with an open heart and an open hand enhances the chances that they will love to be near me and will call or visit me often, because nobody likes to feel obliged or that they need to make a reverential appearance out of duty. That is not to say parents don't make these kinds of low-level innuendos or lay blatant guilt trips on their grown children, but it's not very rewarding on any level. Joy and laughter, without blame or coercion, works best for me.

I delight in my three grown children, and like so many boomers, I am over the moon for my two grandsons. I give love and gifts I can afford, and all my opinions and advice I keep to myself. I am invited often as a result, and I do show up with vitality and joy, because I take care of myself.

How to Have Better Communication

IN MY YOUTH, I learned how to communicate with my romantic male relationships primarily by saying the wrong thing in the wrong tone and always at the wrong time. Yes, for years and years, I felt compelled to inform my close friends, parents, siblings, and for sure the man in my life, the exact ways that they'd hurt me. I was a broken record, and kept repeating and rephrasing their mistakes from every possible angle.

This was my attempt on my part to get them to apologize and then express their love and devotion to me forever. It never happened. Instead, they would get really miffed at me and often storm off. When they left, I could then wallow in self-pity because they'd abandoned me.

I was forever measuring and comparing and keeping score of the amount of loving gestures I gave out to my sweetheart in comparison to what he did for me. I was taken hostage by my low self-esteem, and I succumbed to holiday hype and was continuously living my life in a state of want and expectancy.

I found over the years that men don't respond well to this phrase we gals say: "We need to talk." Men know intuitively that the shame gun is being pointed and is ready to fire at them. There are so many better ways to express concerns and ask for what you want than my old manipulative and hysterical approach.

Thank God I matured and developed healthy communication skills. In my last relationships, men have remarked how calm and collected I am and how they appreciate that I don't need to control or manage them.

This is what I do when I want to clarify things with my honey, my dear husband Ray. First of all, I never ambush him when he comes in the front door. I always wait until he is content and at peace and not distracted. And then I say, "I'm feeling frustrated and confused. Will you be available today or sometime tomorrow to talk some things out?" I'm always polite and inquiring, not demanding. It's also nice to add, "I'm going to be available at 4:30 and at 7:30 tomorrow, if that helps you and works for you."

Some of the simple habits I've found the most helpful when I do want to go over an issue are: When needing to be honest and convey something that I want to change or I'd like to have, I never have a potentially explosive conversation after 8:00 p.m. in the evening. Another one is, I always write out everything that I'm upset about on paper, and then I wait forty-eight hours before sharing it with my mate. I also listen to my gut, and I don't say it or read it or present it unless it feels right. I always ask myself, "Is this forgivable? Is this your problem or is this my problem or is this a friend's problem or someone else's situation to unravel?" Don't play the big-shot teacher, preacher, or do-gooder. If the issue is not mine to fix or manage, it's hands-off.

Waiting the forty-eight hours has a tremendous side benefit. Waiting means you are acting out of choice, not impulse. Waiting puts you in charge of your attitudes, and your words and actions will follow suit. You are self-empowered instead of sliding into the quicksand of self-pity, fear, and abandonment. So choose a time together with your mate and have clarity about which issues you will be addressing and stay on target. Don't deviate or digress.

Use feelings. There are no wrong feelings. Remember, you choose to react and feel. It is not your partner's job who makes you feel anything. You choose to feel anger and take offense, or not. It is always, always you who decides to be hurt or take offense.

Men want to be appreciated and need compliments from us ladies. If you are not praising your man, there are always those women out there who are. The same is true for women—we want praise and you to notice and say something about how we look and dress. Yes, guys. We girls like to be praised as well. Women are always validating each other, and noticing new hairstyles, clothing, etc.

I have listed several love–hate actions because I think if we all could remember these ideas, we could avoid hurting others and appreciate and give each other actions that support our relationships with each other.

What Children Love
From Age 1 Month to Puberty

« Children love to be nurtured.

« Children love to be held, kissed, talked to, in an accepting and nurturing way.

« Children love to play.

« Children love to play make-believe.

« Children love to have their heroes and heroines, kings, princes, queens, and princesses.

« Children love to be outdoors.

« Children love sports, dancing, singing, creating, art, tumbling, and bouncing.

« Children love to be praised.

« Children love to be given treats.

« Children love to be read to.

« Children love to feel relaxed.

« Children love to be special, to feel great, to win, to succeed.

« Children love to be included and honored.

« Children love to feel safe and protected and provided for.

❲ Children love to see their parents hug and kiss.

❲ Children love nature, space, music, singing, dancing, running, and jumping.

❲ Children love to cook, clean, help out, decorate for the holidays, and to decorate their rooms. To participate. To go into adventure. To fly. To ride bikes, horses. To take things apart, or build things. To design things. To socialize.

❲ Children love other kids, of all ages and sexes.

❲ Children love pets, any kind.

❲ Children love hamburger, pizza, candy, and ice cream.

What Young Children Hate

❲ Children hate to be subjected to loud parties or loud music.

❲ Children hate to be cold or left in the sun.

❲ Children hate to be underdressed or overdressed.

❲ Children hate to lose games or to lose pets or to lose friends, family, or a parent.

❲ Children hate to feel bad.

❲ Children hate to feel shamed, feel wrong, feel stupid, to feel blamed.

❲ Children hate to be treated as burdens or slaves, or to feel invisible, or to feel flawed.

❲ Children hate to feel left out.

❲ Children hate to not get picked for the team.

❲ Children hate to witness their parents fight.

❲ Children hate to be given chores or responsibilities beyond their ages.

❲ Children hate to be forced to perform on demand like a trained seal.

❲ Children hate to be compared to their other siblings.

₵   Children hate to feel unwanted.

₵   Children hate to be ignored or unimportant.

₵   Children hate violence.

₵   Children hate to see sexual encounters by older people other than simple affection.

How to Set Up House Rules

THE FAMILY UNIT/HOUSEHOLD is not a democracy so much as it is a kingdom. A kingdom governed hopefully by a couple or a pair of wise, loving, and generous leaders. Our households today are so very diverse, it's difficult to try to even make any suggestion of how best to parent or lead the family unit.

As children grow, I like to see the picture like this: We have little babies, and we often use a small playpen to protect them from pulling things down on them or from touching things or eating things that might harm them. The white playpen mesh siding holds them away from harm's way.

Then the babies get older and we put up gates near pools and staircases to protect them from falling in or climbing up. Then we have fences, and we have a fenced yard that keeps them inside our property's limits and the fenced area. It also protects them and holds them back from running into traffic and unsuspecting parking lot drivers.

So we use these fences and gates until our children can understand the realities of our world. These fences we put up must keep moving further and wider apart, however. Eventually, we open all the gates and set our children, our young teens, our grown-up children free to protect and provide for themselves.

Now the expanding playpen is an absolute must for lots of reasons. If the child or the teen is held back and over-controlled and not allowed some freedom, they will jump the fence, probably too early, and may never return to your home, your kingdom, if you have been a dictator or a selfish, unloving leader.

Now as the leader, it is wise to listen to the needs and wants and dreams of those in your kingdom. Making your home a safe and productive unit is always a direct result of the kind of ethics and principles the head of the kingdom acts on.

I know that it is never a good idea for me to make up rules when I'm angry or in fear. I must wait until I am neutral.

We have many one-parent households, and we have lots of blended families today, and I find that the most valuable ingredient of parenting in any of these cases is consistency. If I can remain consistent, and my children know where I stand and what I call acceptable behavior and what I consider is unacceptable behavior, they know their limits. Children may balk at limits, but I believe that children and teenagers will appreciate the limits that you set, and where and how they fit into the family unit much better than they will by having too much freedom, which leads to confusion.

Consistent and structured lifestyles and a daily routine will actually help the family to have a sense of solidarity. Children with emotional disorders or hyperactivity in particular thrive with structure.

I told my children straight to their faces that they could not have tattoos and piercings if they were living in my house. Now, my daughter did get a tattoo on her lower back and on her ankle after she graduated from UC Berkeley, but one of the things that I suggest to people is to recall just how much they dislike being told what to do. Nobody that I have ever met likes to be controlled, manipulated, or bossed around. Once my daughter had her independence, she made her own choices. I coached a beautiful, mid-thirties woman who had tattoos like sleeves on both of her arms. They went from her wrist all the way up her shoulder. And one day, we were talking, and I just asked her if she had any shame now that she had a teenage son. She was so surprised by the question. She looked straight at me, and she said, "How did you know that?" I said, "Well, I didn't really." And then Rebecca teared up and said, "I regret that I got them every single day. I feel left out and like an outcast everywhere I go. I was so young when I got them. I did not think about getting a job or being a mother."

Often children, teens, can't think that far ahead. Explaining that some choices that they make can't be undone and that the temporary fascination may not be valuable in the long run is not an easy thing for a parent to convey. I recommend finding someone like this Rebecca to share their story with your child and your teen.

Again, open communication and clarity about the non-negotiable house rules and the consistency in carrying out the consequences for breaking a rule will help keep the kingdom, your family, intact. And when the gates are flung wide open, the subjects, your children, the family members, will come back, and they'll come back often and genuinely be happy to be home.

How to Best Communicate With Your Teen, Child, Almost Adult

First, recognize that you have had a divine appointment with your child from their birth. This divine appointment was made by your highest self to ensure your spiritual path so you both could grow tremendously spiritually. Neither of you is better than the other. Show honor and gratitude for each other, and also to your Creator for giving you this perfect package that we've come to call love.

I truly believe that when we can step back from our daily routine and activities long enough, we can find a place of harmony with our teen, and a place of mutual respect, especially because we are a family unit. Once I understood that my children were God's children, just as I am his child, I knew that my role was to support and love my teenagers, and not be their probation officer or their ringmaster. I found when they did have trouble arise, that it's best to just let them know that I see and feel their discomfort and ask if I can be of service in any way. As a parent and a fellow traveler, I can affirm my belief in their complete success and see them as accomplishing wondrous things throughout their lives. I affirm their tremendous gifts, and give gratitude and love and share delight that they are my special, adorable children, and how blessed we are to have chosen each other for this part of our lives' journey.

I never tell my kids they must do this or that because I trust that they have their own path, and have spirit to guide them if they so choose. Listen. I do not take abuse or violence from anyone, least of all my teenagers. My role as a parent is to support, protect, and provide food, clothes, education, and shelter, without controlling them, manipulation, or coercion.

Now, if you have made a mess of your life and are burdened with lots of mistakes and regrets, just admit this to your teen and ask for a clean slate. Keep your mind and your heart open. You may always share your concerns, however, but only once. Let your child experience their mistakes without blame or shame. Ask for permission to give them feedback. Don't just blast at them and tell them what they need to know or what you think unless you ask them if they want to know. Let them be unique. They are not you, and have a different path than yours. Do not let them bully or terrorize you, either. If they do take you hostage and threaten or harm you, then send them away or inform the officials and protect yourself. Stop paying your grown child's bills and rescuing them if they do get into trouble.

If you do send them away, let them know that you love them and you always will. And also let them know that they are not their actions. They are a child of God, and you have faith in them that they will figure things out.

Unless they have special needs due to illness or physical or mental problems, let them know that they need to become self-supporting by age twenty-one. Just for fun, from time to time, just ask how they are. Do not interrogate and constantly quiz them like people do on Thanksgiving. "What are you going to do? Where are you going to go to college? What are you going to do next? What, what, what?" Who likes that? Nobody.

Share your own epiphanies and life wins. Leave your troubles to someone else. Let them have a part in the discussion when making family plans. Don't insist that they go to everything. They don't need to go to Disneyland just because everybody else is. Ask. Encourage.

Praise them daily. Hug them. And play family games, if possible. Cards games, board games like Monopoly, even video games played together create a fun and safe environment to interact with your child at any age.

Your job as a parent is not to win a popularity contest. It is to guide your children, protect and nurture them. You need not be your teen's best friend. The teen years are the years when we naturally need to start separating and individuating from our families, and prepare to start forming our own families and life.

Communication is so important, and it is an art. It is also collaboration with each person in the household being given a voice. Always avoid gossip about members in the household. Let each individual take responsibility for their attitudes and actions toward each other. Treat your role as a parent as a gift, and honor and express your eagerness and happiness to be of service to your family members.

You might even want to give gifts to your child, personalized gifts with notes of praise and appreciation for all the small and large honors they've achieved. Encourage discussion of money and government, and jump for joy at every tiny, creative project they produce or game they win. Do not arrange their lives. Don't insist on public displays of affection in front of their peers. Discuss household rules and chores, and above all, be consistent and loving and direct.

If you do something wrong and step on their toes, tell your teen you are sorry right away. Do not barter, beg, or belittle your teen. Let them wear their hair the way they want. Don't allow drinking and doing drugs in the household, and for goodness' sake, do not party with your teen. Instead, be a good example.

Enjoy your special relationship with this amazing young person. Never compete or compare your ways with your teen's affairs. And don't compare your children to each other. They all have very different circumstances to deal with than you and I did at their age. Openly discuss these differences with an air of humility. You might just learn something. My children opened my eyes in several ways due to what they were exposed to in school, and obviously all the technology they had at their fingertips. It just used to blow my mind. Don't nag, scold, or direct their lives. Let the school of hard knocks do that. Step out of their way. Your life and their life is unfolding.

How Best to Relate and Use Money
The Value of Money,
What Is a Healthy Amount to Give for Holidays and Birthdays

MY PERSONAL BAROMETER for gift-giving and spending, and my love of buying services and material possessions and the privileges I desired from money were highly flawed, if not downright grotesque before I started looking at this and getting myself in alignment with God's will. During my work on myself, I gained a much healthier understanding of my relationship with money and my perceived notions of the power associated by having money or not having it. I also needed to refine my view of my personal worth as a person. I was manipulated by our governments and advertisers to think that money was what would make me happy.

I had a compulsive need, and even a joy, when I was spending money. I did often feel guilty that I was unconscious and frivolous and gluttonous when I contemplated my spending. Just as with the use of food, alcohol, and drugs, the thrill of spending was pushed out of my mind, and I didn't look at it. My yearly gift-giving was so over the top, it was insane. I was raised by a loving, generous mother who gave me everything. She promised me everything upon her death, and the end outcome of this knowledge made me feel entitled and filled my mind with expectations. The only safe expectation I have come to allow myself to hold this day, today, is through God, my Source, my Creator, my Higher Spirit, Divine Intelligence, and Mother Earth or Mother Mary, who also intercedes for me on a daily basis.

Sorting my expectations and my attitude of entitlement has taken me years of introspection and lots of research and humility in order to grow spiritually and away from feeling so entitled. Life has to be the star of everything I try to do. When I celebrate my life and your life, I'm in alignment with God and his mission for me.

One very courageous spiritual mentor a long time ago suggested not giving gifts for birthdays and holidays. Noel was her name. Instead, she shows up to parties and at festivities without gifts, and without any apologies or excuses besides. Well, this proposal was so antithetical to my belief system, I nearly choked and fell over.

That was a long time ago, and every few years since, I get a little closer to achieving her suggestion. However, this is my prescription for a healthy mindset. I am sure many are stingy, penny-pinching, and smugly justifying their ongoing selfish behaviors, but paradoxes do abound when considering each individual's right relationship to money and giving. So I have given less and less. I still have a hankering to buy shiny objects and beautiful clothes, accessories, and such. But when I feel what I call "the call of the wild" to shop now, I postpone the trip, and I think of places and people who have needs that could use some money, and give a little to them—as many of them as I can think of—not just my family and friends, but to organizations that I have confidence in, people who are healthy, people who are helping the planet, or are deprived of the basics of food, health, shelter, and the means to get them.

Success and worth are equated by the degree to which I have grown spiritually today and the amount of self-care and self-love I give myself, and then what I have shared with others.

I had to learn how to receive as well. Learning to ask for payment commensurate with my time and value also was something that I had to practice and learn and get in a right proportion. A large part of my self-worth recipe came from just learning that.

Giving and receiving graciously can be a lifelong pursuit. Being willing to look at this goal consistently, and remaining in action and holding onto an attitude of wanting to change can be made simpler by first getting clarity about your current beliefs and practices. Face it, trace it, and erase it, and if your spending and your belief system are not in alignment with your own standards, you need to change. Ultimately, you answer only to yourself, and if you choose, your personal Higher Power also figures in. The balance of believing in your inherent right for abundance and the willingness to share with others becomes second nature when applied daily. God is my source for love, creativity, knowledge, and money. I reinforce my beliefs and my attitudes by being vigilant in my record-keeping and in my spending habits and my giving habits.

If I do want to give a gift today, I wait and check my budget and give within my means. I give, however, without expectation of appreciation or reciprocation. Clarity and continuity keep fear and worry at bay.

Keep a notebook handy and write down every cent you make and pay out, and on what you spend it, for ninety days. This is a great way to gain clarity. Do the same with how you spend your time. Make no judgments, though. Ask yourself, "Is this what I want?" I still believe I have everything I need and all the time I need. Everything I have ever done is all part of who and where I am today, and none of it was wasted, and I am glad I've taken this journey. Happiness is a choice and a gift from God. Time, kindness, abundance, faith and love, sobriety, a healthy mindset, and a beautiful, healthy body are also my choice. They are also gifts from my Source. Open your mind, heart, and soul, and receive all that has been given to you so far. Source is unlimited and loves to give me and you everything.

How to Face Divorce

THE FIRST THING I want to say is, if you don't know whether to divorce your spouse or not, do nothing. That said, I also know that staying on the fence and entering into a daily debate of "Should I stay or should I go?" will keep you completely insane and unhappy. Be still. Be patient. Ask Source for your guidance.

I also like to write this dilemma on my prayer board, which is a white dry-erase board. And then I thank God for my marriage's calm, serene communication and sanity during this phase of our transition. Meanwhile, if I am not one hundred percent sure that I want to end this marriage, I act as if I am the most considerate, loving wife ever, or husband, if that applies. If I know that I am done, and unwilling and truly can see no hope, or I am clear that I am being abused by my spouse/partner, then I take action to move out or ask them to leave.

I then find legal counsel. I look online for help. I get a coach or I join a support group. Either way, I treat my soon-to-be ex as a person my Higher Power sent to enhance my spiritual journey, and I express in my heart my gratitude to God for the vast amount of knowledge I gained about myself because of this sacred connection.

I hire a great lawyer and ask God to show me how to take care of myself while allowing my soon-to-be ex to do the same for himself.

If you find yourself resenting or re-seeing all the harms your ex has wrought against you, write a letter to your Creator and just give all the facts to your Higher Power. Ask for direction, surrender all outcomes, and sign your name.

The end of a marriage has several phases of surrender. The final surrender, of course, is the dream you shared for your future. Remember, though, love is never wasted, even when we move on from one partner. The truth is, some relationships bring out the worst in both parties. That is not God's will for us to continually hurt each other or fight each other, and it's not good for children to see.

You do each other a spiritual disservice if you stay together for the children. In a toxic union, this is not good. Watching and hearing parents engage and rage is more damaging than adjusting to two households and possibly adding more and new parental figures. Treat yourself with dignity and love. Treat your soon-to-be ex with dignity and love, even if they don't return the sentiment or act nice.

Often, the ego really ramps up its sneaky attacks on us during this kind of stress, especially when our ex replaces us with a new, younger version, or a richer, more powerful sex partner. Your ego will tempt you to think, "I don't want him, but I don't want anyone else to want him, either." Ask God daily how best to be of service to your ex, your fellows, and yourself. Your kids and pets, too, if you have them. Remember, the children and the pets all belong to God, too. He lets you parent them.

How to Cope With the Ugly Truth About Divorce

WE HAVE NO training for marriage and zero training for divorce proceedings. It's important to remember that all love is beautiful, and all energies exchanged in its name perpetuate boundless amounts of joy and give rise to the good of all mankind. Love equals life and community. Conversely, hate equals death and isolation.

The tremendous pain we suffer when we pull ourselves away from the person we once loved and shared our lives with so intimately is an emotional death like no other. Even literal death is oftentimes easier because of its finality. When love dies, there is a period of painful self-reflection, sometimes immediately, and often only after we have thoroughly condemned and mentally assassinated our former mate.

People tend to lean on their buddies to confirm the character assassination of the former spouse in an effort to help their friend sever the last remnant of ties to their ex-partner. I find this practice self-defeating because I never let the scab heal when I do this, because I'm continually reopening the wound. Most people know this to be true, but even still continue to rehash and continue to mentally assault their former love.

The ego is behind this kind of dance of torment and perpetuates the desire to lash out. Songwriters and poets encourage us to claim the utter loss and our personal hopelessness. I lived through this kind of loss only once, thankfully. My suffering was tangible and unrelenting. I silently enjoyed my melancholy as if it were a soul sickness that consumed my thinking until, one day, I decided that I had children who needed me, and I was wasting my precious time for them.

It took me about twenty months to give up my selfish attitudes. I became bored with my own self-awareness and victim mentality. We all take our time to process loss in our unique paces. The more I got into service and submerged myself into helping others, the less I needed to suffer. Support groups can really help a lot, and can expedite the recovery process. Self-talk really seems to streamline the path to personal wholeness, so every day it's important to feed your head kind, loving things about yourself, and ultimately come to surrender that this relationship served a purpose, and that purpose has ended, but the love remained true.

How Best to Part
The Best Way to Part so that Families Preserve Love and Respect, Individually and Collectively

WHEN WE MARRY, we involve not only our partner-to-be, but their family of origin and the new family that we have been blessed to bring into existence. Like every choice we face and get to make, we can go about it from our ego, or from our highest, best self. Despite how our significant other behaves, we account only to ourselves and Spirit and any offspring our marriage may have produced. Our ego has no greater pull on us than when we divorce or when we let go of a relationship. Ego is forever scheming new ways to tempt us to personalize all the negative comments or self-serving, mean-spirited words and actions our scorned partners may hurl at us. I believe to my core that we all do the best we can, given what we know and what society and our government and our spiritual tenets tell us is right or wrong.

I assert that we answer only to ourselves and the God of our understanding. Being polite and respectful during divorce proceedings need not be difficult. It can be quite effortless, if and when we choose to see our journey with our soon-to-be ex as an opportunity to grow spiritually. The lessons you gained can only have been acquired by your involvement with this person you chose. The key is to acknowledge this fact to yourself and your children, family and friends, and associates, that you picked this person. Maybe even pursued and coerced this person to commit to you.

We make choices for lots of motives. The choices made out of fear almost always fail us. We promise forever without really believing in forever. Forever is unknown and impossible, even if it lasts to our own death.

Marriage serves a purpose for some—citizenship, public approval, a desire to be taken care of, and to create children and have your own family. Reality sets in when a couple becomes aware of life's demands and the work and time and money that is needed to survive and possibly flourish in this life. Maturity and compromise may or may not be part of the unit's identity.

The notion of allegiance and the attitude of us against them may not be unified and is often not discussed before the wedding day. Once it has been spoken aloud that one mate wants out, many couples see the white flag not as a surrender but as a war cry. The ego loves a good fight, but has no defense when one mate is determined to remain neutral and declares their desire to make changes in the nature of their dying relationship without malice.

Due diligence will help tremendously to keep the dissolution on track and avoid more hurt feelings.

One or two months after one partner moves out of the home is when the partners begin experimenting with new people. Family, friends, and just about everyone encourage you to have multiple suitors and to "get on with your life.". I suggest waiting a year to really get a handle on your life. Don't criticize your spouse in or out of any of your conversations. I say be grateful for all that you have gained together.

How to Face the Financial Fallout From Divorce

Rarely do couples consider finances when courting, and the consequences of the comingling of their money and that they will acquire assets together as well as each other's debt. Not only do we bring our respective families and their ideas and traditions, we also carry everyone we've ever slept with and all our assets and liabilities, or lack thereof.

Now once the decision to split up in a divorce has been determined and is truly decided, and both partners have agreed to proceed, I really must urge each person to seek legal counsel and do some research into your rights. The more neutrality that can be reached, the better when negotiating about money and assets. By keeping your ego in check, you will realize there is enough for both of you, and you need not be petty or greedy.

The more I can see this person, my soon-to-be ex, in an attitude of gratitude instead of bitterness and fear, the easier the transition will be for us, for our newly single lives.

Sometimes one, or both, has hidden funds and/or assets, and they will try to withhold as much as they can. As much as possible, try to rely on your Higher Power's guidance. I wrote down several questions and asked my Higher Power to work it all out, and I put the list of my questions at the foot of my bed every night, and I expected answers the next day.

My children at the time were eleven months old, my boys, my twins, were eleven months old, and my daughter was around five and a half. And I had custody issues to face, as well as support to work out and a settlement agreement. I knew my ego would want to seize control and try to keep me from facing reality, and from taking care of myself. My daughter and my sons would have to be taken care of.

I had a six-point wish list of what I thought was fair, and so when my ex and I were in mediation, I was calm and clear as we began to work on our individual demands. I like to call mine requests because I avoid trying to demand anything ever now. But then we had our demands, and whenever I say "always" or "never," I am forcing my will on someone. By requesting what I would like or prefer, I immediately step out of the dance of death, aka my will against yours.

Once I ask my ego to step away, I connect with my higher self, God, Spirit, and universal love. When I simply ask what is best for the majority instead of seeking only what I decide I need or insist on, then the atmosphere becomes less contentious immediately, and everyone senses it at once, and negotiations again relax.

I will pause here to disclaim that the ability to feel and understand when my thinking and feelings have been hijacked by my self-centered ego is indeed a slow process. Because even if we grasp this idea intellectually, it often takes a while to travel from your head, that is, your mind, to your heart, which is the doorway to your soul and your highest, best self. The God of my understanding is within each of us, and everything else, whether it is inanimate or not.

There's an absolutely amazing children's book called Old Turtle by Douglas Wood and Cheng-Khee Chee. This book does an amazing job of depicting the idea that God is present in all that there is, all that was, and all that ever will be. I recommend it highly.

Knowing, loving, and trusting in a force, and that this is our source, has helped me to realize and release any fear or the need to control material things. I also understand that this force provides us and me everything I need. When I trust in God, I no longer worry about finances and compulsively desire to obtain outside things to satisfy or distract me from loving my fellows, one and all.

Filled with the knowledge that Source is my source and only true source, I need not pound my ex-partner for pennies, because I know in my heart and mind and soul, there is abundance for us all. It is our birthright to embrace our personal abundance, and there is no reason to try and grab someone else's.

Of course, this lofty concept may not be accepted or implemented by both parties in a divorce. The temptation to try to educate, and thereby force a solution with the soon-to-be former partner should be avoided as much as possible. When I try to convince people to do and act the way I do, I am spiritually arrogant. Source is the only real teacher, and it lets us all come to our own individual spiritual growth at the perfect pace and depth that is right for each and every one of us.

We all grow at different levels and speeds, and it is wise and freeing to allow others the dignity to grow or stay stuck, if that is their true path. Jesus and other spiritual teachers offer us a compass or, if you will, our true north to our most joyous course to self-actualization and our journey to Ithaca.

This is the poem, Journey to Ithaca, and I was introduced to it in my early twenties when I was studying acting from a Greek actor known as Titos Vandis. It basically says, "Enjoy the journey, and don't feel the need to rush it." And here is the poem:

Ithaca

As you set out on the way to Ithaca,
hope the road is a long one,
filled with adventures, filled with understanding.
The Laestrygonians and the Cyclopes,
Poseidon in his anger: do not fear them,
you'll never come across them on your way
as long as your mind stays aloft,
and a choice emotion touches your spirit and your body.
The Laestrygonians and the savage Cyclopes,
savage Poseidon; you'll not encounter them
unless you carry them within your soul
unless your soul sets them up before you.

Hope that the road is a long one.
Many may the summer mornings
be when—with what pleasure,
with what joy—you first put into
harbors new to your eyes;
may not be a Phoenician trading posts
and there acquire fine goods:
mother-of-pearl and coral, amber and ebony,
and heady perfumes of every kind;
as many heady perfumes as you can.
To many Egyptian cities may you go
so may you learn, and go on learning, for their sages.

Always keep Ithaca in your mind;
to reach her is your destiny.
But do not rush your journey in the least.
Better let it last for many years;
that you drop anchor at the island an old man,
rich with all you've gotten on the way,
not expecting Ithaca to make you rich.
Ithaca gave to you the beautiful journey;
without her, you'd not have set upon the road.
But she has nothing left to give you anymore.

And if you find her poor, Ithaca did not deceive you.
As wise as you'll have become, with so much experience,
you'll have understood, by then, what these Ithacans mean.

—CONSTANTINE P. CAVAFY

How to Heal From Divorce

LOVE IS AN amazing feeling, and the height of all life experiences. Congratulate yourself for risking and reaching out for it. It takes courage to remove our barriers and our veils of tears and all our lofty aspirations.

I recommend yoga and meditation. Change your diet. Try something totally new. Get up and stretch every morning, and write on Post-its: "I am loveable." "I am fun." "I am amazing." "I can." "I have it." "I give with open arms."

Look at yourself and smile, and greet yourself with a friendly look in the mirror every morning.

Ask yourself where you'd like to travel to this year.

Wear bright colors or unusual accessories.

Change your hair.

Fellas, grow a beard or shave your beard off.

Step out your front door or back door and take in the day.

Have a healthy breakfast.

Ask Spirit to guide your thinking and actions and show you how you can be of service to others.

Try a new hobby or take a dance class or martial arts class.

Keep a journal.

Join a new group.

Avoid eating lots of junk food, sugar, and drinking alcohol.

Ask for guidance from God on what your body needs to run smoothly.

Call one, two, three friends each week and set up things to do with them.

Volunteer at senior homes and visit the elderly.

Go to the children's section in the hospital. Bring them toys.

Enjoy your autonomy and peace of mind.

I find it helpful to shake all my blues away by jumping up and down and shaking my butt and arms and hands and legs.

When my Lhasa Apso, Tao, passed away, I went out and got a new puppy, Jessie James. A mini, sixteen-pound Australian shepherd.

Connect online and go to meet-ups near you. Get into the groove of life.

Time will heal your wounds. Jump back into life with vigor and vitality, even if you don't feel like it. Do it anyway. Your mind and body and soul will sync up eventually.

How to Avoid Choosing the Same Person Wearing a Different Hat ... After Divorce, Onto the Next

I HAD TO learn the hard way that it is always better to take time off from dating once my divorce was final. I know lots of people who don't even wait until they are legally divorced. I did take two years before dating after my husband passed away suddenly. And that wait gave me an opportunity to understand what I wanted and hoped to find by being in a relationship. I asked myself, why do I feel that I need a relationship? This "why" changes as we get older.

My first marriage was for a romantic fantasy about love and had no real goals other than playing house together. My second marriage to my high school sweetheart was to start my own family and build my own family traditions. I looked for someone who was safe and hardworking, who would be a good father and a good provider. He was all of them. Passion, although, wasn't necessarily that big of a want at the time, I thought.

My third marriage was about finding mind-blowing passion and someone with the same interests as my interests. None of these motives was particularly bad, but they were all about what they could give or do for me. I am now happily married to a man who is whole and complete. He is my passionate lover and my best friend. We complement each other and share each other in our various pursuits, and our union lets us enjoy life and adventures as a couple.

My relationship with Ray was not by accident. We both knew what we wanted and sought to find it. All the men who I had engaged with before were found randomly. We met in a group or in school or a play production or we worked together. I never really knew what I was looking for, and did not take any real time or effort to understand who or what they stood for, or what they were focused on, or what they wanted to accomplish in their life. Red flags would pop up, which I promptly would ignore. Mean streaks, self-obsession, or workaholism or sloth were common traits. Big egos with little to no self-worth or self-care were also very typical and modeled after me, as well. Not guiltless, here.

If you want to stop repeating the same mistakes and learn to move slowly and continue to progress slowly while you get to know and witness how this person you might be dating reacts and operates, please wait three months or more before having sex together. It takes that amount of time to see and hear how another person thinks and behaves. It's funny how we will study and research to buy a new car, go to a class, take a trip, what investments we're going to put our money in and grow our wealth, yet the very essence of who we are is often short-changed in favor of getting our sexual needs satisfied. No research required. No study. And no due diligence.

If you take time to write about your last relationship and what worked and what didn't, write also what you learned and how to use that info to find and create your new love–sex relationship. There is no need to rush, and remember, you have the right to get what you want. Watch your date and how they take care of themselves, how they handle stress, loss, and their emotions. How they get their needs met. How they are with money. How their health is, and whether they take care of themselves. Are they comfortable with you doing your thing and thinking things that they don't always agree with? How do they handle conflict, loss, pain, and success or failure? Then ask yourself, how do I? Am I ready to love someone? Do I need some personal work to fully love myself?

Remember, two wrongs don't make a right. Water seeks its own level. You will attract someone as healthy or as sick as you are.

What do you need to change about yourself, your thinking, your standards? Work out what you did wrong in your previous romantic relationship. Take ownership of your part and ask your Higher Power to assist you when you are open to love again. You will be open again. Believe me.

Be ready and awake and go on dates without expectations. Just be observant and listen. Keep your personal life protected until your gut tells you this is a safe person.

In order to truly find the perfect mate, you must come to peace with your parents of origin, too. This peace is gotten by finding acceptance and ultimately forgiveness for their failings, and gratitude for the gifts you received from them. There are always gifts, even when people hurt or disappoint us. The acceptance and the forgiveness you embrace does not in any way minimize or condone or justify their sick or bad behaviors in the past. It means you have to let the pain and suffering go, that's all. When people hate their parents or their siblings, there is unfinished work to be done. If it is left unaddressed, you will find the damages transferred to you. You must face it, trace it, and erase it by asking your creator to remove it.

How To Be Fully Prepared To Say Good-bye
When Your Parents Walk On

WE ARE NEVER really ready when one of our parents dies, even if they are very sick and very old and hanging on to life by a thread. I have two very helpful suggestions that will really help you to feel love and peace and complete with each parent, no matter how rocky your relationship throughout your life with them has been. A minister once told me that I would never find my true-life partner unless I was at peace with both my parents. I thought this was sort of a negative message at the time, but as I grew older, I understood why being okay with each parent would help me to choose a partner and live contently with them.

Lots of people feel so guilty when one of their parents dies, because they basically abandoned or ignored their parents because of old hurts and resentments. They just stopped visiting or calling at all. Some of us really feel it is our job to keep our parents alive. This is often the case of adult children of addicts and alcoholics, because their parents essentially told them it was their job to do so. At the end of the day, it will hopefully be easier to view your parents as people that parented as well as they knew how. This is in no way an attempt to erase or minimize the poor, neglectful, or even violent behavior or unkind words. It means they don't define you by their mistakes. You are the way you are and they gave you some good and bad input.

Here is a little recipe for freedom from remorse and regret...

All throughout your life, about every three to five years, please write and give your parents a list of your ten top favorite memories of each of them, individually. And on their anniversaries, please write one about your ten top favorite memories of them as a couple. Don't do this if they are not together, however. That would be seen as a guilt trip.

Use your senses—your smell, sight, touch, hearing, taste—and only write ten memories. There is a magic in number ten. You'll see; it has more impact.

You can write it on really nice paper and tie a nice ribbon around it, or you can frame it. Do something that you know that they would enjoy. I gave my mom one on her 75th birthday and framed it for her bedroom. She sadly didn't want her age listed, however, so I took off the number 75th and left the "Happy Birthday" part. Keep your ideas brief and simple. It works better. Believe me, it is very healing to recall specific moments with my only mother and daddy. I did the same kind of favorite memory list for my father, Roy. My list of memories of him included when he was baiting my hook when we went fishing. I described how his freckled hands looked as he deftly tied the special bass lure hook on to the end of the line and cast for me…it always made me feel proud and love for him. Another warm recollection was when he put me on the top of his shoes and danced with me at the Petroleum Club and I could smell his Old Spice aftershave. My mother got her list and lived another twelve years more. I read my dad's list to him at his bedside in the hospital the night before he died. He had been pretty incoherent the prior five days, but perked right up and smiled and nodded with each memory I shared. No regrets and nothing left unsaid.

Two of our secret longings in life are to have been seen and heard. If you get a bit of gratitude thrown in, that is the sweetest of all.

The other little suggestion I offer up is to do something creative for each parent. When I found out my dad had cancer, I painted a tee-shirt for my pop that said "Roy's Fan Club."

I drew it freehand and then painted it on a banner with the faces of our family and pets behind the banner. I am not really an accomplished artist, but the act of making this tee-shirt helped me to accept the reality that my father's life would be ending. He had been given three months and lived another eighteen.

I will switch gears now and reveal another priceless activity that I perform to keep my sanity and serenity. The next idea is my famous prayer board. My board is a dry-erase board to be purchased at an office store. I use many colors of dry-erase ink on my board. Originally, a dear friend shared with me how she used her board and how miraculous her results were. Being stubborn, as I am, I did not go out and get my first board for another five years after she'd mentioned that to me. In the beginning, I had five columns on my board: one for a list of my fears, one for my resentments, one for the things that I felt powerless over, one for prayers for people, for my family, friends, and myself, and one column was devoted to my gratitude list. I continued writing on my board like this—but now I have two—for the next seventeen years. I had to develop a code, though, because it was available to view, and my husband would sneak and look at it.

After I became a widow, and I moved further north to Novato, California, I got a new way to use my board. I was living alone, so I dropped the board idea and began writing on my bathroom shower doors and all the mirrors in large letters and bold colors. I guess I might've looked a little kooky. I wrote thank you notes to God for things that I wanted to happen or to manifest in very detailed, specific terms, and always in a positive manner, never using any negative terminology. The more detailed and the more descriptive, the better, and always as if the positive outcome had already occurred.

This works. It really, really works. If you believe it works, it does. It didn't work for the person that shared this with me. It works for me, and now I take requests from my family and friends, and if I hear about someone's challenge in life, I put it and them on my two big boards. I am remarried and feel it is not considerate to use all our common mirrors and our shower door to write up my requests. My writings are automatic and flow. I only put something on the board once, and then I let it go. It is uncanny how well this works. I guess because it is intuitive, in essence. I never want to write for anything that hurts, or takes anything from someone else.

The next thing I want to talk about is Expressing Gratitude. Raising my three children, I got in the habit of writing letters of appreciation and praise for their birthdays and any awards and any graduations or personal achievements that they got. Love letters, really. What was really fun is that they wrote some to me. Yes, they expressed their love and gratitude to my family, my friends, and on Mother's Day, they would each write a letter and place it in a silver monogrammed box with their names and date, saying "To Mom."

Today, they send texts, and they attend events where I am being honored. They remember my sobriety birthday. They witness my life and see and hear and appreciate me.

Write your love notes to your kids, friends, parents, and to yourself, and always remember to write love notes to your Higher Power.

How to Make Your Ten Top
Favorite Memories for Each Parent

WRITE OUT TEN memories or type them as a list.

The reason to do this is that if you don't express your love and gratitude before your loved one's death, you will be very upset that you didn't and find it hard to forgive yourself.

Think about what people say when they lose someone suddenly…I never got to say good-bye, or I never got to tell them how much I loved them, or how much I appreciate them, or got to thank them for everything they gave me or did for me…

Even when we know people are sick well in advance of the death, it still is always a surprise, so why not make the effort as soon as you can.

Your favorite memories need to have a sensory component to bring them alive and truly engaging. It is a snapshot in time—a moment that springs out of your fuzzy recollections. Make them juicy and fun and happy. You are letting your dear one know you witnessed their life, you felt them, smelled them, heard them, watched them, appreciated their work, enjoyed their creations...

Describe as vividly as possible how you felt when you think of that moment or hour or day with them...

You will both truly enjoy this small but mighty trip down memory lane. If the parent has already passed on, go ahead and do it anyway and create a formal ceremony of your own fashion and deliver your tribute anyway. Just do Ten Memories...it is the perfect amount.

I have known a few individuals whose parents were so evil or entirely unknown or were never involved in their life. I don't think it is a good idea to try this for parents that fit this profile.

This is an exercise of sharing with the people you really do love.

My Seven-Step System: How to Finally Find the Love of Your Life

My seven-step system is an all-inclusive process that will get you the results you've only dared dream of before. Each step is designed to build onto the next. After completing half of these steps, your dreams will cease from merely being your secret fantasy to your finally understanding and believing the love of your life you're longing for will be yours actually. It will actually happen.

I created this system from years of experience coaching men and women who were disappointed, demoralized, and downright fed up with their dating experiences. Some were even disgusted by their own lame love choices in the past. So here are the steps, and I will go into them a little more in-depth:

Step 1: Define what you want.

Step 2: Evaluate your readiness and check your motives.

Step 3: Revise needs and make sure they are realistic and that you have attainable goals.

Step 4: Build your mindset and lose any doubt you may have been carrying.

Step 5: Create a want ad for the universe, not to print, and also to construct a strategy and a plan to meet your loved one.

Step 6: Prepare, practice, and poise.

Step 7: Support, sorting, and sex.

The reasoning behind **step one**, defining what you want, is that I've found that most individuals are truly vague on what the "want" is that they do want. It's almost as if people are expecting to walk out their front door and trip over the handsome prince or exquisite princess sitting on their doorstep. I must confess that movies and fairytales that I read as a child also led me to this magical thinking. In this age of being able to see and meet online, we don't need to hope to find our love, and we don't need to sit and wait. No, we actually can put ourselves into the best position and be ready for love.

I know also that what we want changes depending on our age at the time we are looking. Someone who's twenty-four has a very different want than a woman, let's say, fifty-four years old, seeking a partner. My system will aid you in your discovery process. The exercises I give and my probing inquiries will shake the fairy dust away long enough to find your ideal path. We will keep the other fairy dust for you and your true love to dance in together when you find each other.

So let's talk about **step two**, which is to evaluate your readiness and see if you approve of your motives. In this step, we can make certain you are sure-footed as you set out on your true love journey. Why waste precious time by finding out midway you are just not really ready for love? What does being ready for love mean? How do you know you're ready?

These questions are deeply personal and require my assistance and practiced ear and considered experience to navigate you through. During our conversation together, I will take your hand as we look closely at your "whys." Your "why" will determine your search's success or failure. I intend to help you uncover and approve of your why so you save your time, money, and energy. This is how you raise your odds for love success. By the way, my notion of success is always based on love, primarily on my love partnership with a mate, followed closely by my love for my children, my parents, my friends, associates, and of course my dear four-legged friends.

Step three: revising your needs and getting real. In this important process so far, we have gotten a lot of worthwhile information and are ready to begin drawing the outline of our masterpiece. We have clarity on what we want and why, but now can determine if it is what we need for the big picture. Is it really going to be worth it once we get it? Will it fulfill our life goals and make life thrilling and happy?

This takes us to **step four**: building your mindset so you don't sabotage your efforts and can joyfully call in your rightful true love. This step could easily keep you stuck in limbo without me as your guide to your self-love. What could take a lifetime, we can accomplish in no time. I have self-worth and self-love and self-honoring techniques that will set your heart love on fire. You will radiate and glow with inner strength and peace and seduction. You will no longer feel the need to diminish yourself. No more shyness or self-awareness to block the glory of who you are. Because you will be shining so brightly, you will attract the same brilliance in your true love. You deserve the best, and our work will build your confidence.

So now we're on **step five**: crafting your want ad and constructing your map and strategy for your true love crusade. Now, by this time, I've helped you know what you want, know why you want it, approve of what you want, believe you are worthy to have what you want, and now I will assist you to write out specifically the exact qualities and attributes you seek in your partner. This process may seem awkward or somewhat too controlling and lead to unrealistic expectations. Not so. As I guide you through the previous steps, your authentic self will have been perfectly conditioned for this endeavor. I find that taking some private time in an undisturbed place and simply assuming the position by sitting with a pen and a pad of paper, that your list of wanted qualities will flow from your intuition without hesitation. The qualities you desire will reveal where and when to place yourself in order to meet the kind of person you seek, as surely as it will reveal where to avoid looking. We don't want you wasting your time "looking for love in all the wrong places" ever again.

So now we're at the **sixth step**, which is preparation, practice, and poise. Now that you are clear on the who and the where, we will set the stage and pick the best attire, wardrobe, and pamper ourselves by preparing our outer package. Now this is a very subjective step. Diets, haircuts, wardrobe, needs to be right in order for all the other work we've done to be showcased properly.

Practice. This is begun by showing me and other clients, if we're in a group, a sample of outfits, etc. And once you've accepted dates (notice I said "dates," plural), you try out different styles of attire as well as different types of people to date. Dating is, in essence, a fact-finding mission. Dating several different people is typically a "new" thing for most people. Multiple dating activity allows us to behave the way we prefer to act when we do meet our true love.

Poise. This describes the serenity and the inner calm and cool we feel even when our heart is jumping out of our body because we have found the one. We need this poise in order to take care of ourselves. We need this poise to avoid train wrecks.

The final step, **step seven**, offers support, sorting, and sex. Support is the feedback you'll be given on your various dating experiences. Honest, noncritical, kind feedback will be greatly needed and appreciated. The support from me and others in a group, if you belong to one of my group sessions, will benefit you immensely and help you remain confident and consistent, and help you eliminate any negative habits or behaviors you discover.

Sorting. Multiple dating allows you the luxury of remaining

detached until you find your true love. Once you know your presence and your time and your energy are valuable and a true gift to all you "spend your time with," it will be easy for you to sort out the persons you do or do not want to spend your priceless time with. The opposite is also true. If you don't have "the feelings" for someone, it is easier to let them down when you remember you don't want to waste their precious time, either.

Finally, the last step. We come to the last part of the seventh step: sex. We will agree and plan on when the timing is right to introduce sex. For some of us, it's often been way too soon. And that's because we've used sexual encounters as a way to have intimacy because we are afraid to know each other. But in this course of dating, we'll discover if your relationship needs to be mutually exclusive, and if it is contingent upon commitment or not, and when to commit or leave. This is not a cookie-cutter decision, by the way. Sexual activity is a highly individual need and has a different priority for different people.

So that is my seven-step system to finally find the love of your life. I hope you will give me a call at 855-288-2744 to sign up for your Brilliance Breakthrough session with me, complimentary. And please go to my website, which is www.CoachDeborahD-owney.com. If you have further questions or need any kind of information, please email info@CoachDeborahDowney.com.

To All My Sisterhood: Sex and Intimacy Solutions (SIS)

THE DESIRE FOR intimacy and sex is a normal and healthy human drive. But a lot of women, even maybe the majority of women, often feel that sex is dirty and ungodly. Well, I feel that a lot of women also view the difference between sex and intimacy as quite blurry. In fact, sex equals intimacy. That may even be the standard opinion these days.

Sex can be the glue that holds a couple together, especially through conflict or loss, but sex is not supposed to be used as a net to trap and manipulate a new hostage. Most women need to feel safe with their partner in order to feel vulnerable enough to surrender their bodies to their lovers. Women need not fear saying no to sex. We are not designed to be doormats and people-pleasers. We do own our bodies, and we can have sex if we want to, but we shouldn't do it because we think we're going to be punished by our love mates if we refuse. Our bodies belong to us, and are a gift from our Higher Power to be enjoyed at our discretion, not by coercion.

The discovery part of each relationship is exciting. It's fun, and it's a time when we're discovering our interests. We're seeing who this person is. It's often very intoxicating because we are very focused on each other. We're enthralled, if you will. But to build real honesty, you need intimacy, and these things take time.

So how do you create intimacy? I know most women, myself included, must enjoy the person. I must find them fun to be with. I want to know what they like and what they don't like. The main thing is that I need to come to like this person a lot. I need to enjoy this person. I need to watch and see if there are red flags—things that I would be uncomfortable with on a regular basis.

When a person interacts with another person, our animal instinct to merge with this person will take over. It's subtle, but it happens, especially if we're consistent, we keep having contact, and we're flirting. Well, over time, this will lead to taking each other to bed, and this can be tricky. You need to know who the person is that you're sleeping with. Even if you say you're not going to sleep with someone, if you keep going over to their place and having private meet-ups with them, especially if the meetings are secret or private, you're creating just the soil for sexual expression and lust to grow in. So the bad news is that I have to be responsible for my sexual behavior for myself, of course, but also for my partners—the partners that I have in the future (any of them, whether I stay with the one that I'm currently with or not).

What we're talking about here is life and death. I must be responsible and get my AIDS test and ask for any other sexually transmitted diseases to be checked as well, because no one else is going to protect me. I must not be timid with my partner. Instead, I strongly advise that questions be asked upfront. This is merely a precaution to not fall head over heels and jump into bed knowing very little. They're very much a stranger, and you want to know about your sex partner before you have any such situations. We are talking about life and death, as I said, ladies. Women need to love their own bodies before they can be put in a compromising position with a veritable stranger.

I know there is an inherent desire for excitement and passion, knowing how quickly and deeply most imperfect women respond after sharing their precious bodies with a new partner, showing no self-restraint. But using self-restraint will yield far more beneficial and satisfying long-term relationships. Most women hate hearing this, but it is kind of a fun period if you don't tell the partner anything about it. You just know you don't want to go into the sexual arena until you're in the driver's seat, ladies. It's up to you to take care of yourself and make sure that they get tested, that you're tested, that everybody is ready for this, and that there's no other people involved, like wives and husbands and so forth. People don't tell the truth sometimes, and so I need to make sure, and yet not be obsessed over the process.

Waiting a minimum of ninety days to date someone without having sex allows a lady just enough time to see if there are enough reasons to move forward in a relationship. Developing intimacy slowly and consistently will make your first lovemaking experience even more erotic. For all new couples, this is true. I don't suggest you announce all of this to your new partner initially. But I do feel that women would benefit everybody if they waited. The notion that I have to have sex in order to be sexy is simply not true. The people of our planet, Earth, are all entitled to find their true love. The questions that need to be answered are: How long since you had an AIDS test? How many other people have you slept with? When did you last have sex? Are you married, or are you in another sexually active relationship? Have you thought about making our relationship exclusive?

What you don't want is surprises, ladies, and dishonesty, which can lead, of course, to your death, and the death of anyone else with whom you are sexually active. We don't like to think about this, but that's true. If you are in a new, monogamous relationship, and your lover is an alcoholic or an addict, well, you must ask these questions as well. Even after you've been in the marriage for a while, you may have to ask again.

Loving an alcoholic, or an addict, or both, if they're active in their disease, you will be affected by moods. He will have mood swings, depressions, selfishness, self-pity, and anger. I also include untreated bipolar people in this category; they're just as hard to live with and to date. Loving such people is possible if you take care of yourself and keep the focus on your needs, and continue to love and encourage your partner without using sex as a punishment, a reward, or by withholding it or manipulating with it. Remember that their disease has nothing to do with you; it is not your fault, and you cannot control it in any way. Do not take their moods and bad behavior and ugly words personally. They're not about you. They're always about them.

Think twice before you marry an alcoholic, if you've figured out that they're actually a practicing alcoholic or addict. They will break your heart because the chances for their sobriety are slim. They will promise you time and time again that they will stop drinking or using, but they may not. You have to take care of yourself.

Sex accompanied by loving words and kindness is the basis of the ultimate intimacy that women seek. Only adding in a spiritual component, like sharing prayers together, can eclipse the sensuality of tenderness, because praying is so personal. The urge to merge is a God-given impulse, and is therefore inherently good. It can be erotic, sharing this part of who you are with your lover. Again, check your motives for wanting sex and being disinterested or uneasy about engaging in sex if you haven't been interested for a while. Men don't consider sex equal with intimacy or love the way women do. Men experience intimacy when they feel heard and admired and appreciated. When a man knows he has pleased his family, people in his kingdom, he feels satisfied. Holding hands, rubbing your honey's back or feet, stroking their hair, their forehead, rubbing their back and shoulders, showing true curiosity about his work and his interests, and knowing what he is yearning for all confirm your love and affection.

Intimacy Quiz

HERE IS A list of questions that will help you identify the things you use to keep yourself away from trying to meet people:

- ❮ Do you worry that there's no one out there for you?

- ❮ Do you fear you that you've missed the boat, that there's nobody left ?

- ❮ Do you tell yourself that all the good ones are gone or taken?

- ❮ Do you wonder to yourself who would want me, I'm such a mess?

- ❮ Do you fear your looks won't attract your ideal mate?

- ❮ Do you tell yourself that dating is stupid and that you find it annoying?

- ❮ Do you tell yourself that you like not having to answer to anybody, that you are happy being by yourself ?

- ❮ Do you tell yourself you're too old ? That everybody wants someone young, not someone your age?

- ❮ Do you fear that you won't be interesting enough because you lack higher education or you are too poor or too wealthy?

- ❮ Do you tell yourself you just don't have any time to date....it's too much work!

- ❮ Do you tell yourself to just play it safe because you don't want to get hurt again...like the last time?

- ❮ Do you secretly wonder who'd want me... I'm a mess?

- ❮ Do you think I am way past the perfect age to find my life partner?

- ❮ Do you feel afraid to date people because you are really timid and shy?

- ❮ Do you hate to meet new people, to converse mostly because you inwardly feel you have nothing interesting to say?

All these negative statements undermine the actions we can take if we let them. We don't have to let our egos beat us. I will teach you and guide you on how to escape your worry maze. The good news, friends, is that you can and will find the Love of Your Life with my coaching. Plus, you will have fun doing it.

Coaching Quiz

❮ Do you feel like there is something wrong with you?

❮ Do you find it difficult to stand up for yourself?

❮ Do you feel like you always pick the wrong person for love?

❮ Do you keep making the same mistakes over and over?

❮ Do you feel stuck, overwhelmed, and confused?

❮ Do you regret the choices you've made in your career, marriage, location, and health throughout your life?

❮ Do you fear growing old and facing death?

❮ Do you stress out about everything?

❮ Do you secretly feel unworthy for love? Or success?

❮ Do your children terrorize you, take advantage of you, disrespect you, lie to you, steal from you, and or abuse you?

❮ Do you lack direction, enthusiasm, passion, and purpose?

❮ Do you pray, meditate, write, and still feel pissed off and suspicious on a daily basis?

❮ Do you dread going to work?

❮ Do you hate confrontation?

❮ Do you say yes when you'd rather say no?

« Do you feel you're too old?

« Do you ask yourself, "Why me ? Why did I get sick and diagnosed with…?"

« Do you feel bored and uninspired?

« Do you feel victimized and misunderstood?

« Do you fear you won't have enough money to last through your retirement?

« Do you self-medicate and relax with drugs, alcohol, overspending, watching TV all day or every night, gambling, reading, working, exercising, traveling, eating, knitting, collecting things—cars, bikes, jewelry, anything?

« Do you push yourself to perfection?

« Do you feel superior, inferior, or have opted out of the game?

« Do you procrastinate and then beat yourself up?

« Do you separate, isolate, or need to be constantly with people?

« Do you like how you look?

« Do you take care of your body, emotions, mind, and finances?

Let's get you going. Jump onto my Love Express. My Love and Dating Academy is ready to board and your True Love is waiting. Call 855-288-2744 or go to my website www.CoachDeborahD-owney.com and sign up for your FREE Brilliance Breakthrough Session.

Affirmations to Counter Negative Thoughts

I HIGHLY RECOMMEND affirmations, and I have written some here to just sort of jumpstart you writing your own. So please, have fun with this, and write things down that feed your soul and give you what you need to counteract anything that you say or do or think that makes you go into the negative. Here's the first one:

- ❩ I keep my power and my wits at all times. I am calm, clear, confident, and courageous all day long.
- ❩ I feel fantastic, free, head to toe.
- ❩ I fall asleep easily and sleep peacefully all through the night.
- ❩ I wake each morning feeling grateful and eager to do my best in work, play, and to learn more about myself and how I can serve my family and friends, my fellows, spirit, and, of course, myself.
- ❩ I research all important decisions and find all the answers I need to make the best choice in every situation.
- ❩ My actions, attitudes, beliefs, and dreams are in complete alignment with my authentic self.
- ❩ I am loved, give love, feel and receive love, with open arms and an open heart and soul.
- ❩ Prosperity, peace, and purpose lead my motives and produce perfect harmony in all my endeavors.
- ❩ I focus on the big picture and let Divine Intelligence handle all the details.
- ❩ Spirit inspires my creativity and fires up my imagination.
- ❩ I let other people take care of themselves while I take care of myself without guilt and the need to control.
- ❩ I have all the time and resources to live life with gratitude and passion and love until I walk on.

« When I get frustrated with any kind of technology, I leave the area and step outside. I remember that my happiness and well-being are not dependent on technology. They are dependent on my Source.

« When in confusion, fear, or doubt, I relax and wait for clarity. I can also ask for help.

« I am okay not knowing everything. I like being vulnerable and teachable.

« It feels great to help my fellows, and equally enjoyable to let others teach me.

« Every day is a new opportunity to love myself and those I encounter.

« I take care of myself by being honest with myself and requesting my needs as they are relevant.

« I am responsible for my attitude, actions, and my words.

« I give myself whatever amount of time I need to accomplish any task that is important to me.

« People love being around me. I share my thoughts and listen closely to what others want to share with me.

« It is okay for me to disagree with you, and it's okay for you to disagree with me.

« Laughter is like singing to my cells. It shakes all the dust out.

« Music is intoxicating. I make time to listen to all kinds of music so I can better understand my world and all its cultures.

Hobbies & Vision Work

I AM A sensuous being, and I get inspired by my sense of smell, touch, and taste, and what I hear, and what I see. Over the years, I've developed my ability mentally to see beautiful images in my mind and visions of myself walking, singing, running, and visiting the ocean, and even flying. This all helps me, because I have multiple sclerosis, and I could see myself limited and envision the worst. Instead, I use these images that are clear, and sometimes they're abstract, to help me.

I practice yoga and tai chi to help myself still my mind and calm my nerves as well as strengthen and help my balance. Knitting and needlepoint work is another thing that I do, because I'm a woman and I want to be in touch with my feminine side, and the simple, slow conversation that women enjoy in work like that, which takes me out of my masculine side when I work. And it also helps me simplify my thoughts and bring me into the present— the moment.

Learning to master my thoughts and savor my gratitude and my joy has helped me to dispel all the ugly or destructive or habitual or trance-like thoughts that wind up being useless. This is a practice that I highly recommend for you to find on your own— something you enjoy, that puts you in the zone, as long as it's not alcohol or drugs or food or sex or something that just makes you go numb and escape. No, something that calms you, is pleasant, makes your mind slow down, and helps you remember whether you're a man or a woman, and enjoy it.

Three Steps to Let Go of Guilt and Shame

I WAS DIAGNOSED twenty-four years ago with multiple sclerosis. I was thirty-four years old. It was a challenge to stay positive and not sink into self-pity and be in constant fear of my future, and I had a tremendous amount of shame and felt like spoiled fruit. Definitely felt separate and defective. To be ill meant I was weak and imperfect in my family's eyes.

I have helped myself and will share my discoveries and how to deconstruct all my inner demons in this writing. The first part of this conversation, I want to define what I mean for our purposes. I want to use two of the dictionary's definitions of the word "guilt."

1. Remorseful awareness of having done something wrong.

2. Self-reproach for supposed inadequacy or wrongdoing.

Both of these definitions confirm that guilt is a feeling that I create with my punishing mind. My ego has weighed the evidence, and I have been found guilty. So guilt is something I go to when I go ahead and self-proclaim my mistaken thinking or behavior and keep focusing on my mistakes over and over and over in my mind.

Now I'd like to define "shame" so we can understand this idea a little better. I'd like a clear framework with which to reveal the options that I've come up with for dealing with these two conditions.

When I'm feeling shame, this is the best description that I have found for that definition: a painful emotion caused by a strong sense of guilt, embarrassment, like scandal, or unworthiness or disgrace. A loss of honor, respect, or reputation. The second definition is "a great disappointment."

Wow. This is another aspect of shame or a deep regret. For our conversation in this writing, I'd also like to point out, let's agree that guilt is primarily self-inflicted, while shame is less about what was done and more about how I see myself.

The other use of the word "shame" falls into causing someone to have feelings of shame. So I can actually inflict shame on other people. The steps I use to coach clients out of shame and guilt are to excavate, evaluate, and elevate. In order to excavate, I like to dig deeper. I get a sense, I explore my sense of guilt, and it comes from deciding we have made a mistake or failed at something and/or not lived up to our own standards. I like my clients to really get clear on exactly what the guilt is stemming from, because our ego is always trying to find some way for us to justify our actions so we are right, and also feel in alignment so we think we're good. It is only when we can't logically excuse ourselves that we have no recourse but to take on guilt.

The second step in my process is to evaluate my standards, to see if they are truly my standards or inherited standards from spiritually bankrupt people, what I call "tormentors"—larger-than-life egomaniacs that demand perfection and have unrealistic standards that are impossible for anyone to accomplish. Now that is where false guilt is created, and we measure our behaviors or success or so-called failures by tormentors, people who are unkind and feel the need to belittle and/or withhold love and approval, and are perpetually demanding impossible goals. These tormentors were likely raised by parents that were shamers and blamers, too.

Let's say you did lose control and said or did or did not act when you could have, but didn't out of fear. Ask yourself, well, if Sally or Tom or XYZ had done this, would this be forgivable? And if this were done by a child that did this, would it be forgivable? Then ask yourself, "If I knew then what I know now, would I make the same mistake?" And if your answer is, "No, I would do things differently today," why are you beating yourself up for something that you didn't know? I mean, if you didn't know it, and you didn't know better, why do you keep blaming yourself for something you didn't know?

Now we have excavated and found the reason for the guilt or shame and determined through our evaluation whether this is, in fact, our own personal guilt or some other strong, dominating person's we want approval from. Now here we are at the point of elevation. This is the part of the process where we see how we have a choice to see the benefits of an incident and to lift up the incident as a needed blessing for our awareness and our personal growth. I find that when I ask myself, "Is this forgivable? Am I trying to perform an insane goal?" Even if I truly did mess up, I need only to take responsibility and admit it—admit my error to those I have affected.

All of this process takes place in my mind, and I rely on my Higher Power, my higher self, to take my fear and guilt. I write out a letter to my Higher Power and spill my guts and ask my Higher Power to help me let go of my guilt.

Shame is something others can put on me. Shame can also be for someone else I love. I elevate the end result as a true blessing that's providing me insight and awareness for my growth. So there are many facets to shame and guilt, but sometimes it's other people's shame and guilt. We need to be very clear on whose guilt we're holding, whose shame we're holding, and if we're looking at something in a way that is not productive, it is up to us to see the blessing, to find the blessing to take the time to evaluate it. So my steps are: excavate: dig deep; evaluate: look at the motives, look at what you knew, whether it's forgivable; and elevate: see this as a necessary part of your growth in your spiritual path.

Outline of Five Steps to Transform
Any Area of Your Life With Ease

MY PROCESS WILL shift you from doubt, fear, confusion, and worry to clarity, courage, confidence, and faith. Awareness, Attitudes, Action, Acceptance, and Accomplishment.

The first step is awareness in my discovery process. So many of us are stuck because we can't see how we are self-abandoning by our vagueness in important areas of our thinking and behaviors.

My client, Sarah, was very unhappy in her marriage, yet in our initial discussion, she really was not able to verbalize her apathy, much less connect it to her feelings of loss for her deep desire for intimacy and her need to be touched and for sex from her husband. By working with me, she did get the clarity, and we were able to start putting her back on track and use the next four steps to regain her passion, and she and her husband made huge strides using my re-energizing techniques—holding hands, backrubs, my seven-day sex challenge—and I also got her to name it, claim it, and dump it.

Step two is attitudes. Once I identify the trouble source in step one, I have a clearer idea of the goal we need to work toward, so I check with my client to see if her attitudes or his attitudes have become boulders that come between them and their goals.

One such case was a man named Tom and his parenting skills of his moody, secretive son. When Tom and I worked together, he discovered he had this attitude towards his son which was controlling, and he was in fact an interrogator, which was motivated by his fear and ego. This of course pushed his son away and made him unresponsive and unwilling to be close to his father. By working with Tom and his son, Johnny, we were able to develop shared interests, and Tom continued with his coaching with me with the remaining three steps.

The third step is action, in my transformation process, and it has to do with taking action. I have helped my client to be aware of the root problem in step one, and reviewed and improved their attitudes in step two. We have clarity and courage now to move into action. Most of my clients have not looked at their behaviors from a benevolent witness before working with me. This is a process where you look at your life somewhat like watching a movie, and seeing the various stages that you've gone through.

So getting clarity on what they have been blocked by and see-ing how their inner critic has bedeviled their thinking, most of my clients are often dumbfounded when we ask what their motive is when they tell me about their plans and the actions they want to take. It is the wise person indeed who can honestly look at a motive for an action before moving forward.

The reason it is wise is that if a motive is petty or self-serving or dishonest or greedy, the end result will be unpleasant or a downright disaster. The idea of taking care of myself and not putting myself in a position to be hurt is revolutionary for most of my clients. I ask myself before I act or speak, "Is this kind? Is this the truth? And is this necessary?" If it's not all three, I stop myself in my tracks. I find this self-reflection process extremely valuable because it saves me time and money and hurt feelings and resentments.

One lovely lady I was helping with a recent breakup comes to mind. Cheryl had had several relationships with older men and bad boys, too, and men that were still working to get their busi-nesses off the ground. Basically, all these men were not ideal for Cheryl. She had herself together. She had money, a great job, good health, and lots of loving friends. Cheryl did not need a man to complete herself. She was on her game. Like many times before, she had found herself feeling like she had to do all the work in a relationship. Cheryl had not held off on sexual relations, as we had talked about several times. As soon as she broke up with someone, she very quickly got into something else. She had not let her men pursue her. For Cheryl, waiting seemed unnecessary, and then she suddenly got it. She realized it was fear of them losing interest that had made her jump into bed too soon with just about every man she'd been with. Now she was mad and ready to tell her current boyfriend a thing or two. She asked me if I thought she should call her boyfriend, Steve, and tell him how selfish and immature he was.

When I asked her why, what her motive was, what she wanted to accomplish by doing that, she burst into laughter, saying, "Oh my God, you're right. It was me all this time. I gave myself away, and then I blamed them." Her only motive was anger and a desire to scold this doof she had picked. Sometimes the action is to do or not do something, or not say something, or to say something. When in doubt, pause and reflect and ask yourself, "Do I need to take this action?" I want you to trust yourself. If you are not coming from fear, greed, anger, or control, take the action. Take the risk. Be prudent, though. Do a little research. Take care of yourself, and mind your own business.

The fourth step in this process is acceptance. Acceptance does not mean agreeing with or signing on to something or someone else's behaviors or attitudes. No, acceptance in our process means non-resistance. Think of a boulder in a stream. The rushing water flows past the boulder, over and around it. It does not resist the boulder. It remains intact. The boulder stays still, and the water flows over it. I have found that which I resist, persists. I like Walter Cronkite's approach when he'd end each show and say, "And that's the way it is." Unfortunately, the universe knows when we really do surrender and stop our inner fight and demand things go our way. It's uncanny, really. The moment I truly accept what is instead of grousing, whining, wishing, and hissing, and bitching that things would turn out the way I want, that's when things actually do change. I told you I'm sober twenty-three years. I also was diagnosed with multiple sclerosis that same year, so to be clear, acceptance does not mean I like my MS and I'm resigned to my fate and stuck with it. No, I don't suck it up. No, it means I understand the situation, and what I can change, I change. What I can't change, I deal with one day at a time.

Accomplishment is the fifth step in our process. This is where abundance and happiness is an inside job. Affirmation. Once I let go of blame, shame, fear, anger, and control, I have so much time to use to accomplish my dreams. The very fact that I have reflected truthfully and become accountable to myself is an amazing accomplishment, and my life improves.

The crazy thing is, as I get honest with myself and embrace all of my brilliance, and face and work on all of my failings, I am now overflowing with a deep desire to share myself with an abundant and generous heart.

SECTION 5
About My Practice

Why I Chose Diamonds in the Rough as My Company Name for My Coaching Practice

I HAD A hypnosis session with the idea of clearing away any and all obstacles for the upcoming opening of my cabaret theatre some years ago. My hypnotherapist took me down several levels of consciousness and thought, until I was enveloped in this Technicolor, bountiful, beautiful garden, where I was walking through, as I remember, feeling light and joyous, exploring and discovering all the exotic, blooming flowers that lay all around my feet. I heard birds singing and felt the warmth of the sun on my arms and shoulders and the back of my head. I felt full of energy and excitement, like a child searching for an Easter egg.

In the heart of the garden, I saw this bright, shiny object tucked by the side of an evenly rounded rock, shaded by the dainty leaves of a freesia. I bent down to get this object and saw it was this amazing, huge, round, perfectly cut diamond. My therapist at the time told me that that diamond was me. She suggested that I recall this scenario, this scene, right before I walked onstage, and to feel the power and be the radiant diamond for all to see.

Now I am retired. I'm retired from acting and singing and performing, and I feel as if it is my deep calling to help others to discover their worth. It is my honor and privilege to help cut away anything that hinders my clients' achievements, and give them the ultimate clarity and help them find their true brilliance.

This requires skill and patience and creativity on both our parts. The hurts and abrasions of life can be cut away, and the remainder of the gem, being you, can be buffed and polished to increase the brilliance as often as needed. Diamonds are strong and cannot be destroyed by fire or rain. A diamond's worth is always increasing and can be highly enhanced or diminished by the setting that it's in. Our job is to find the perfect setting and keep looking and polishing until we discover that setting we know to be our true home. Worry is a distraction from our path and robs us of our most precious tool, that is, our time and our attention. So my book is here to help you find and spend your time and find your highest potential.

Why Coach With Me?

Who coaches with me? What kinds of people have sought me out? Well, this is just an example of the list of types of people. Doctors, plumbers, teachers, artists, film directors, marriage family counselors, nuns, mothers, young and old, teenage girls, lawyers, hairdressers, singers, graphic artists, college students, masters' students, coaches, business coaches and health coaches, dancers, film producers, police officers, baby boomers of difficult, uncooperative senior parents, nurses, office managers, optometrists, grandmothers, grandfathers, financial advisors, accountants, family members over a grief of a loss of a loved one, people with newly diagnosed illnesses, film art directors, children of alcoholics, parents of alcoholics, writers, musicians, foresters, mail carriers, cinematographers, psychiatrists, fashion designers, and notary publics.

Performance Anxiety is another area of coaching I offer to my clients for all their creative endeavors. My forty-five years as an entertainer/ performer/producer has given me lots of insights and coping skills I can share with you. If it's a boardroom presentation, a stage production, a television interview, or being the main speaker at the local chamber of commerce, I can help you feel great and get your point across with style and clarity and a heap of confidence.

I began coaching by helping actors prepare for auditions and to get them ready so they'd be effective for job interviews and get booked for the part.

With all my spare time (tee-hee), I helped my mother run and manage two retirement homes in Santa Monica. My thirty-five years of hands-on experience with elders has given me much to offer with regard to getting the best services for their elder parents. I help the baby boomers understand just when and how they need to take care of themselves in the process as well. I guide both parents and boomers to stay sane and happy. Showing them how to love each other and celebrate the end-of-life transition is very worthwhile for me as well as them… the process won't be scary any longer.

I am a real estate investor as well and learned that business from my very successful and highly regarded (by other investors and bankers especially), dearly departed mother. I can assist clients to find the best strategy to use to stay on top of the market and find and honor their risk tolerance.

I have been a successful small business owner for over three decades. My experience allows me the great pleasure of coaching new, budding women/men entrepreneurs to build their dream businesses.

I am also a coach for newly diagnosed multiple sclerosis patients and the chronically ill. I myself was diagnosed twenty-three years ago with remitting relapsing MS. I subsequently learned how to take care of myself while developing a profound level of faith in God. My personal daily spiritual practices have fostered compassion, courage, and strength for me to take the best possible care of myself. Helping patients, and in turn their caregivers, maintain personal dignity and truly embrace life and all its joys… is perhaps my true best life's purpose.

I became a certified chemical dependency counselor sixteen years ago. I help parents of addicted and/or troubled children (or adult children) find recovery-based solutions. I have worked with families of alcoholics and addicts all over the U.S. for twenty years. I understand firsthand the fears and helplessness parents feel when their child is in trouble or drinking/using drugs. I offer hope and a tried and true system of techniques that reunite the family. We focus on the family unit and become co-creative partners in the recovery process. The tone/atmosphere and home environment shifts from secrets and aversion and/or control to a place of mutual trust and encouragement. Love and fun are returned to each family member.

No matter what, I go on and continue to grow and expand. I give motivational talks on all the above topics at special events and would be delighted to speak at your event or your group. Please go to www.coachdeborahdowney.com. You can call 855-288-2477, my toll-free number, and claim your Brilliance Breakthrough session by going and opting in to my newsletter and signing up for your Brilliance Breakthrough session.

Thanks for reading my book.

 www.twitter.com/debdiva123

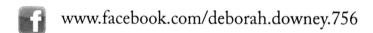 www.facebook.com/deborah.downey.756

www.linkedin.com/deborah-downey/68/8ab/679